D1124666

Organizational Misbehaviour in the Workplace

Organizational Misbehaviour in the Workplace

Narratives of Dignity and Resistance

Jan Ch. Karlsson

First published 2012 by
PALGRAVE MACMILLAN

Palgrave Macmillan in the UK is an imprint of Macmillan Publishers Limited,
registered in England, company number 785998, of Houndmills, Basingstoke,
Hampshire RG21 6XS.

Palgrave Macmillan in the US is a division of St Martin's Press LLC,
175 Fifth Avenue, New York, NY 10010.

Palgrave Macmillan is the global academic imprint of the above companies
and has companies and representatives throughout the world.

Palgrave® and Macmillan® are registered trademarks in the United States,
the United Kingdom, Europe and other countries.

ISBN 978–0–230–29679–4

This book is printed on paper suitable for recycling and made from fully
managed and sustained forest sources. Logging, pulping and manufacturing
processes are expected to conform to the environmental regulations of the
country of origin.

A catalogue record for this book is available from the British Library.

A catalog record for this book is available from the Library of Congress.

10   9   8   7   6   5   4   3   2   1
21   20   19   18   17   16   15   14   13   12

Printed and bound in the United States of America

Contents

Part III Concepts

List of Tables and Figures

Tables

Figures

Preface

What first made me interested in workers' and managers' resistance in the workplace was a programmatic article and research overview of Western Europe (Edwards, Collinson and Della Rocca, 1995). It was a brilliant article in many ways, but it was not its brilliance that caught my attention first; rather, it was its shortcomings when it came to analysing resistance in my homeland, Sweden. The authors claimed two things: resistance is 'relatively unusual' (p. 303) and the political climate is such that research on this topic is 'virtually unthinkable' (p. 285). My reaction to the first claim was strongly negative. My early experience as an industrial worker and later on as an academic told me that they were wrong. In fact, I have never been employed in a Swedish workplace where there was no resistance. The degree and forms of resistance have varied, of course, but there have always been some activities like these going on. The article also made me reflect on what I had heard from other people about resistance. I remembered all the vividly related events that my sister, who is a trade union leader, had told me over the years; the stories that my friend, the welder, had amused us with during our fishing trips; and what my wife had revealed about life at the libraries where she had worked. The assertion that there is virtually no resistance in Swedish workplaces is, I was convinced, simply wrong.

My reaction, therefore, was that I had to initiate a research project in order to investigate resistance in Swedish workplaces. In this, I needed a grant from a research fund. However, according to Edwards, Collinson and Della Rocca, it would be impossible to obtain money for such a project in Sweden, and I was inclined to agree with them on that point. It was true that Swedish research into resistance was almost non-existent. To my surprise – and to the credit of the Swedish Council for Working Life and Social Research – I received a grant, this book being one of the concrete products thereof. (For reports from the project dealing with resistance and organizational misbehaviour in Sweden, see Huzell, 2009; Lundberg and Karlsson, 2011; Strömberg and Karlsson, 2009.)

The thank-yous could be extensive, but I will keep them to a minimum. I do not know Edwards, Collinson or Della Rocca personally, but I must thank them for provoking me into entering this field of research; Stephen Ackroyd and Paul Thompson for discussing some early ideas with me, something which made me change some of my lines of argument; Marek Korczynski for making me aware of another song for Chapter 29; Elin Johnson for Chapter 60. Margaretha Strandmark for helping me orientate in the literature on bullying and harassment; Andrew Sayer for thoughtful and very helpful comments on Chapter 1; and Chris Warhurst for brilliant comments on all the theoretical chapters at one of their later stages. But most of all, I thank my project comrades, Henrietta Huzell and Susanne Strömberg, for the wonderful collaboration.

Jan Ch. Karlsson

Acknowledgements

Permission has been granted for selected use of material from the following:

From Helena Lundberg and Jan Ch. Karlsson (2011) 'Under the Clean Surface – Working as a Hotel Attendant' *Work, Employment and Society* 25(1), pp. 141–48. Reprinted by permission of Sage.

From Jörg Kirchhoff and Jan Ch. Karlsson (2009) 'Rationales of Breaking Management Rules – the Case of Health Care Workers' *Journal of Workplace Rights* 25(1), pp. 457–79. Reprinted by permission of Baywood Publishing Company.

Part I
Organizational Misbehaviour

[T]he extent to which workers consent to production is a concern seen through the eyes of management. Dignity is the concern of workers, it is the goal of their behaviour, and it is our concern here.

(Hodson, 2001: 60)

1
Dignity and Autonomy at Work

People need dignity and autonomy at work. If we are denied dignity and autonomy, there will be a strong tendency for us to resist our working conditions and misbehave at work. The bulk of this book is made up of stories or narratives on this theme (Part II). In this chapter, I introduce the theme by discussing dignity in relation to some problems that employers experience when organizing work, as well as some of the consequences that follow on from the tendency to organizationally misbehave, that is to break organizational rules. Following the narratives in Part II, I suggest a new way of conceptually analysing these phenomena (Part III).

Philosophers have been debating questions of dignity for thousands of years. However, there is one thing that they seem to agree upon: dignity is extremely important to people – it is a matter of human worth. Where work in particular is concerned, dignity is crucial in order for this activity to be meaningful and satisfying – and this is independent of the worker's gender or ethnicity (Hodson, 2002). At the same time, the dignity of workers often conflicts with the economic demands of efficiency, productivity and profit. For employers, it is more important that their employees' work is efficient, productive and profit-yielding than dignified. For the workers themselves, dignity is usually just as important, often more so. For employers, employees are resources for profit or efficiency, while for employees, employers are resources for making a living under dignified conditions.

In the social sciences, it is argued that dignity at work should at least imply 'the ability to establish a sense of self-worth and

3

self-respect, and to appreciate the respect of others' (Hodson, 2001: 3). In Hodson's analysis, there are several conditions that can counteract dignity at work. One involves the power position that employers have vis-à-vis their employees, something that can be abused by subjecting the latter to invective and contemptuous treatment (Bies and Tripp, 1998; Vredenburgh and Brender, 1998). Bad management and misrule can be included in this category as these make working conditions even more difficult. It would be a mistake to regard organizational misbehaviour as always being in opposition to the efficient organization of work. Several of the forthcoming narratives bear witness to employees going to great lengths to protect productivity and work flow from bad management. A second condition is excessive work. Today, working demands have been intensified at many workplaces to the extent that they obstruct dignity at work (Burchell, 2002). The curtailment of employee autonomy creates a third dignity-threatening condition. Autonomy does not mean total independence, but some measure of influence and control of their work is something that most employees strive for, while employers often want to safeguard it as their own privilege. In Britain, for example, there is a clear empirical trend towards 'a considerable decline in employee task discretion' (Felstead, Gallie and Green, 2004: 163), an important aspect of autonomy. Finally, when employees work in teams, contradictions may appear in regard to employee autonomy. If teams are formed 'from below', there are opportunities for them to involve a real increase in employee responsibility and control. However, they are often set up by employers and initiated from above, which means that incentives for work intensification are built into the organization: the team members are supposed to push each other to work harder (Thompson and McHugh, 2009: Ch. 24).

It seems reasonable to me to suppose that the different ways of denying workers their dignity can give rise to organizational misbehaviour. Employees seek dignity in many different ways, as testified to by the narratives in Part II. It is possible, however, to take the notion of dignity at work further (Sayer, 2007a: 567): working conditions that provide employees with 'integrity, respect, pride, recognition, worth and standing or status, are positively related to dignity', while conditions that result in 'shame, stigma, humiliation, lack of recognition, or being mistrusted or taken for granted are negatively related to dignity'. Again, it does not seem much of a leap to suppose that employees who are subjected to negative conditions will try to restore their dignity, or that those enjoying positive conditions will try to maintain their dignity – in both cases through organizational misbehaviour. Still, the quest for dignity can be expressed in rather undramatic terms, as in this example concerning restaurant kitchens:

> Like all workers, cooks attempt to 'get by'. They do not demand paradise but strive for a passably smooth routine.... Cooks wish to transform a potentially oppressive environment into a regime in which they can live, and from which they gain a measure of satisfaction. (Fine, 1996: 20)

However, it is seldom an all-or-nothing affair (Bolton, 2007: 8–9); certain parts of the work can provide dignity while other parts do not.

At the centre of dignity lies autonomy (de Terssac, 1992). In the words of Ackroyd and Thompson (1999: 74), 'the tendency to seek autonomy is endemic'. It is also well substantiated that employees both want autonomy and influence at work and feel that management blocks their attempts to obtain a stronger voice (e.g. Cully et al., 1999; Freeman and Rogers, 2006). Further, the trust of others is an important part of having autonomy. If employers trust their employees – to be competent at their jobs, to be conscious of their responsibilities and to perform their work well – they will give them autonomy, and thus employees achieve dignity at work (Sayer, 2007b). If, on the other hand, employers do not trust their employees and instead organize their work on the premise that they will always have to be supervised and controlled, the employees will not be given autonomy. Under such conditions, we can expect that there are strong forces that drive organizational misbehaviour. At the same time, we must be aware that autonomy is seldom gifted by employers, instead being won by means of resistance.

It is important to note here that what I am talking about is how things are in practice, not what they are said to be. In John Roberts' (1984: 296) words, it is 'the difference between what is *said* and what is *done*, and though a person through words can present a favourable version of his or her intentions, this version will only be believed if it is embodied in the way they act'. If, for example, an employer propagates a corporate culture that emphasizes responsibility and influence, but still strongly superintends and closely measures the employees' performance, there will be little trust and autonomy. Sayer (2007a: 575–6) clearly expresses this gap between what is said and what is done:

> If employers make pronouncements about treating everyone with equal respect, but in their actions, and in the conditions which they provide for their employees, treat them unequally, then their words are likely to be seen as hollow, as being contradicted by their deeds. Expressions of equality of recognition which are not backed up by equality of treatment and distribution of resources, including job security and the provision of working conditions are likely to appear hypocritical.

Many of the forthcoming narratives about organizational misbehaviour have their background in such cases.

In the remainder of this chapter, I argue that there is a wealth of knowledge about what characterizes dignified work, but that this knowledge is not enough for all work to have those qualities. The reason for the problem is employer dilemmas inherent in wage labour versus human dignity. If the demands of dignified work were entirely compatible with employer interests, such knowledge and policies of dignity would not be necessary. Dignity cannot be a means to an end for solving employers' dilemmas, as is postulated in the often searched for but seldom proven (Judge et al., 2001) positive correlation between work satisfaction and job performance.

Dignified work

Working-life research shows quite clearly what qualifies as dignified work, while influential political organizations have formulated policy documents with demands for decent work and quality work. I have already quoted Hodson's (2001: 3) summary, saying that it is at least a requirement that workers can feel self-worth and self-respect, as well as respect from others. Another formulation that I have referred to is that dignity can arise under working conditions that result in 'integrity, respect, pride, recognition, worth and standing or status' (Sayer, 2007a: 567). Two of the most widely known policy lists of characteristics of dignified work emanate from the

International Labour Organization (ILO), a United Nations agency, and the European Commission (see the overview in Bolton, 2010). They are intended to lay the foundations for working-life policies and contain similar criteria. At the level of the labour market, there should, for example, be good employment opportunities without discrimination and a balance between work and the rest of life. At their workplaces, employees should have decent hours and a safe working environment, and there should be social dialogue and worker involvement.

More systematic – and perhaps also more concrete – discussions of criteria concerning dignified work can be found in working-life research. Let me mention three examples: socio-technical theory, the control–demand model and the dimensions of dignity at work model. Socio-technical theory has had a great impact on both the theories and practices of the organization of work. The basic idea is that there are two systems at a workplace, the technical and the social, and these must be kept in balance (Herbst, 1971: 12; my translation): 'If one optimises the technical system at the expense of the social, the results will be suboptimal. The same thing occurs if one tries to optimize the social system at the expense of the technical.' Instead, it is a matter of attaining a 'joint optimization' of both systems. An important part of the social system is the demands that employees can make on the content of their work. Einar Thorsrud and Fred E. Emery (1970: 194), two of the most influential scholars of the socio-technical school, specify workers' needs in this way:

- the need for job content to be reasonably demanding in terms of other than sheer endurance, and yet to provide a minimum of variety (not necessarily novelty);
- the need to be able to learn on the job and to go on learning (again it is a question of neither too much nor too little);
- the need for some minimal area of decision-making that the individual can call his own;
- the need for some minimal degree of social support and recognition in the workplace;
- the need for the individual to be able to relate what he does and what he produces to his social life;
- the need to feel that the job leads to some sort of desirable future.

These formulations are rather guarded – 'reasonably demanding', 'minimal area', 'minimal degree', 'some sort of'. However, if they were to be fully put into practice, working life would look quite different from how it does today. Workers and managers would enjoy more dignity in and at work.

The background of the control–demand model, developed by Robert Karasek (1979), is that there were two influential but independent theories in the field of the psychosocial effects of work environments on employees. One concentrated on work demands that lead to stress while the other studied employee decision latitudes and influence on work. In each of these traditions, there were research results that seemed paradoxical or inexplicable. Karasek's great achievement was to bring these two theories together in a single model, containing high and low demands in relation to high and low worker control at and over work. The result is a typology of jobs or work environments: these can be passive or active, low-strain or high-strain. The basic idea is that qualities of work environment are a function of the specific combination of demands and control. On this basis, it is possible to create a hierarchy of jobs from good ones to bad.

– Active: high control and high demands
– Low-strain: high control and low demands
– Passive: low control and low demands
– High-strain: low control and high demands

The really good jobs are those that combine high demands with high control; that is the active ones. Then comes a type of job that is fairly good as it also contains high control, namely a low-strain job. Jobs characterized by low control are bad ones, while high-strain jobs are worse than passive ones as they also contain high demands. One important characteristic of the theory highlights the balance between the demands put on a worker and that worker's possibilities of handling these demands. Two types of relations are involved. One is when demand and control diverge, which is the case when demands are relatively greater than the worker's control; the other is when they match each other. Later, a third dimension was introduced, namely social support from workmates or superiors, which can function as a buffer and make bad jobs a little better (Karasek and Theorell, 1990: 68–71). The model has been confirmed empirically in many studies in many countries, showing, for example, that bad jobs are correlated with heart disease (Karasek and Theorell, 1990: Ch. 4). Karasek's message is clear: all jobs should be active because bad jobs endanger employee health. However, not all jobs are good jobs.

The third and final example of knowledge of what constitutes dignified work has been put forward by Sharon C. Bolton. Building on a number of former models, she presents one of dimensions of dignity in and at work, underlining the importance of the dimensional construction of the model (2010: 166):

Thinking in terms of dimensions allows for a detailed analysis of dignity at work that covers many important issues in the world of work and how experiences may differ. For example, many people enjoy dignity in work as they have some autonomy and/or meaning in the type of work they do, but not dignity at work in the sense that they do not enjoy good terms and conditions of employment. Yet others may carry out mundane and monotonous work but benefit from dignity at work in that they gain from a physically healthy working environment and secure terms and conditions. Combined, a dimensions of dignity model represents a useful opportunity for a holistic analysis of work in its blend of the inherent dignity of the human person with people management policies and practices that may either support or deny this human condition.

The dimensions of dignity in work are that the worker should have autonomy and a job that provides job satisfaction and is also meaningful, while at the same time giving the worker respect and opportunities for learning and development. Dignity at work means that there are structures and practices that give the worker a healthy work environment, just rewards, an individual and collective voice, job security and equality of opportunity. It is obvious that not all work is dignified.

These three examples indicate that there is a rich fund of knowledge concerning the qualities of dignified work, while the examples of the policies of the ILO and the European Commission are signs of important international organizations' ambitions regarding working life. However, far from all, work is dignified. It is not because we do not know enough about dignified work that all work does not have those qualities. It is not because of a lack of policies either. Why is this knowledge not used to a higher degree in practice? Why have the policies of these influential organizations not been implemented to a greater extent? What are the mechanisms that are so strong that they can block this knowledge and these policies?

Problems in organizing work processes

Organizational misbehaviour emerges in the relations between the mechanisms of effective, productive and profit-yielding work, and dignified work. Against the backdrop of employees' tendencies to defend their dignity, the employers' task of organizing work processes is not an easy one. The relationship between dignity and resistance is not only a general, moral and philosophical issue; it is also a very concrete dilemma for employers when it comes to organizing work. Thus it also has a real impact on employee conditions. When we use the concepts of employer and employee, this entails talking about the work form 'wage labour' (Karlsson, 2004). The social basis for wage labour is that people possess labour power, which in a classic formulation is defined as 'the aggregate of those mental and physical capabilities existing in a human being, which he exercises whenever he produces a use-value of any description' (Marx, 1998: 242). In wage labour, people's labour power is hired in and hired out on a specific market – the labour market. It is in these two bases for wage labour – labour power being part of the human being and labour power being hired on the labour market – that the answer to the question 'Why is all work not dignified?' can be found. It should be observed that this goes not only for capitalist wage labour but also for other types of wage labour, such as when labour power is hired by public sector institutions, independent and voluntary organizations, and households (Furåker, 2005, Ch. 2). That is why I contrast dignity not only with profit but also with efficiency and productivity, which are primary employer concerns in all kinds of wage labour. These concerns lead to a strong employer interest in controlling employees' work and the whole labour process.

In social science analyses, it is sometimes said that, in terms of historical development, there are three main ways for employers to organize work (Edwards, 1979): direct control through supervisors, bureaucratic control through rules and regulations, and technological control through machines. A different idea is that there is a dialectical oscillation between direct control and a type of organization in which workers have a certain degree of responsible autonomy (Friedman, 1977). It is difficult to uphold any idea of a linear development of work organization. When looking at any organization, it is most likely that we will find traces of different organizational principles, like archaeological layers. Organization analysts can learn a lot from archaeologists.

Behind most analyses of this kind lies the thought that human labour power has two sides that employers have to allow for. The problem is that these sides have quite contradictory characteristics. On the one hand, human labour power has clear advantages in the form of the power of initiative, skill, adaptability and creativity. It is important for employers to make use of this. On the other hand, there are disadvantages in terms of this power being held by people with a will of their own and who do not at all, perhaps, want to direct their capacities towards what their employer wants; they might even be unfavourably disposed towards such demands (Friedman, 1977: 78). An expression of this is one plant manager's troubled reflection on an organizational change (Taplin, 2001: 16):

> He said that when you give workers more control then you have to accept that they might not always use it to your advantage. 'We spent almost two years empowering workers, then the last three years trying to regain control over their work output. It seemed the more control they got, the higher our costs went.'

It is important that the employer is able to foster the workers' cooperative creativity and restrain their subversive creativity (Linhart, 1982): employees can use their creativity in the service of their employers, even to the extent that they break organizational rules to improve production – 'cooperative transgression'; in doing so, they try to 'remedy the mistakes, the dysfunctions of the system' (1982: 95; my translation). But they can also use their creativity to contest the rules in order to protect their dignity – 'subversive transgression'.

Generally speaking, employee consent to, and cooperation with, employers are in need of explanation, as much as conflicts with and resistance to them. When there is cooperation, it is often established through management and workers agreeing on the basis of quite different rationales – in my terms, efficiency, productivity and profit versus dignity. The relationship between conflict and cooperation can thus be organized in different ways (Edwards, Bélanger and Wright, 2006: 130–1). It is possible to say that conflict comes more naturally to workplace relations than cooperation due to the involvement of human labour power – and thus dignity.

It can rightly be claimed that employees are in an inferior position in relation to the power of their employers. Pollert and Charlwood (2009: 345), for example, say that 'All employees are vulnerable in that they are part of the wage labour relation with a much more powerful employer.' There are, however, a number of problems, dilemmas and contradictions that employers have to deal with as a consequence of labour power being a human power. In one analysis, taking this as its point of departure (Lysgaard, 2001), a distinction is made between the technical–economic system and the human system of employees in workplaces. The technical–economic system is made up of the work organization, its hierarchical structure of positions and its goals. All employees are part of this system and the system demands a lot of things from its members in order to achieve high efficiency and profitability. The human system is defined by the way humans are constituted. What is at stake is the individual's interests as a human being and, since the bearer of labour power is the human being, he or she is also part of the human system. But these workplace systems are in opposition to each other, placing individual employees in a very difficult situation as they are part of both systems. First, the technical–economic system is insatiable when it comes to the employee qualifications and skills that it has a use for, such as industriousness, strength, concentration, reliability, competence, creativity and loyalty. However, humans cannot work indefinitely, nor do they have inexhaustible strength, and so on. Human beings are limited vis-à-vis the insatiable demands of the technical–economic system.

Second, the role that the technical–economic system assigns each employee is specialized or one-sided. It is a rather narrowly delimited area that the employee is expected to be unceasingly occupied with at work. At the same time, human beings are many-sided, having a lot of action tendencies and development needs. If I am hired as a welder, the system's only interest is that I keep on welding. It is of no importance that I am good at fishing for salmon, that I like book binding and that I would like to learn lace-making. Finally, the technical–economic system is implacable. It is not in the interests of the system to keep a certain person employed if he or she can be replaced by someone (or something) that serves it better. But such precariousness is demanding as employees as human beings seek security.

The insatiability, one-sidedness and implacability of the technical–economic system collide with the limitedness, many-sidedness and security-seeking of the human system. For the employees, the dilemma is that they have to be members of the technical–economic system if they want jobs, but this goes against being human. A solution to this dilemma is to make sure that they obtain protected membership of the technical–economic system by building a buffer between the two systems. They establish this buffer by constructing a self-organized counterculture in the form of a worker collectivity, which can be used as a weapon to defend their human dignity and to gain some autonomy at work.

There is, then, a strong tendency for employees, and especially workers on the lowest level of the workplace power hierarchy, to form a collectivity to defend themselves against the demands of the work organization. For the employer, this is a real dilemma. The employer needs to establish what Lysgaard calls a technical–economic system; however, at the same time, this risks triggering mechanisms among the employees that create a counter-organization, a worker collectivity that forms the basis for resistance and organizational misbehaviour. All this because labour power is part of the human being.

Another problem for employers results from the same phenomenon: employers cannot purchase already-completed work on the labour market, only the right of disposal over their employees' labour power. The reason for this is that labour contracts cannot specify in detail what tasks the worker is to perform at work, how to do them or at which pace. Thus the relationship between the workers' efforts and what they get out of them cannot be decided in any detail in advance. This creates a fundamental indeterminacy, to use Baldamus's (1967) term, involved in the labour process. There are two types of indeterminacy (Smith, 2006): one concerns the worker's efforts while the other concerns labour mobility – the production indeterminacy of labour and the mobility indeterminacy of labour, respectively. Further, there are also two aspects of the production indeterminacy of labour (Furåker, 2005: 80–1). First, formal or informal agreements between employee and employer are subject to changing circumstances in, for example, technologies and markets. In doing so, the agreement becomes obsolete from the perspective of one or both of the parties. Second, the employer's knowledge of the details of the labour process – what is to be done, how it is to be done and so on – is incomplete: only the workers have an intimate understanding of how best to perform their work. Mobility indeterminacy means that the workers can quit their present job and go to another employer. This possibility is, of course, subject to the state of the economy and the labour market, but the option is always there in principle. Any work contract is therefore temporary and incomplete.

From the employer's perspective, this creates the problem of having to bargain with regard to the indeterminacies: effort bargaining and mobility bargaining. Instead of the employer having control over hired labour power, there is what has been called a 'frontier of control' (Goodrich, 1975) between employer and employees – a moving frontier influenced by the constant formal and informal effort and mobility bargains occurring at the workplace and in society at large. This is why another metaphor is so appropriate, namely the workplace as a 'contested terrain' (Edwards, 1979). In this way too, the employer dilemma is constituted by a conflict that is built into the very relationship with the employees.

Because of labour power being a human power and because of the indeterminacies of the wage labour contract, there is a strong incentive for employers to exert control over their employees. This tendency does not, however, result in any specific empirical pattern of work organization, as employers always have to consider the dilemmas that the characteristics of human labour power confront them with. At the same time, the control interest of the employers causes a corresponding mechanism to emerge on the part of the employees, that is, a strong incentive to establish and keep their dignity. Neither does this tendency result in any given empirical patterns; however, organizational misbehaviour is one possible outcome. The employers' greatest problem is that the labour power they need to employ is inherent in people. This creates many dilemmas that permeate workplaces and pave the way for organizational misbehaviour to become a common feature of working life.

Organizational misbehaviour – an introduction

Seeking dignity when it is under threat is the main mechanism behind employee resistance. Problems that employers encounter when organizing the labour process pose many kinds of threats to dignity at work. The reasons for these threats can vary from superiors bullying individual subordinates to relations between capital and labour. Forms of resistance can vary from cynical thoughts about a boss to a full-on class struggle. These forms of resistance are various empirical manifestations of the dignity mechanism, depending on which other mechanisms are present and active (Danermark et al., 2002).

In the social sciences, there are several ways to describe and analyse organizational misbehaviour. In Part III, I contribute to the field in two ways: first, by presenting an empirical analysis that helps to answer questions about which rules employees draw on when breaking organizational rules; and second, by suggesting a model in which organizational misbehaviour is the overriding concept, while other concepts – resistance, abusive supervision, collective discipline and private business at work – are subsets thereof, defined by their relation to the hierarchy of command in the workplace.

In the present context, I simply wish to warn against a concept that expresses a whole perspective that is strongly value-laden, namely 'resistance to change'. The bias that lies behind this term is that management always takes rational decisions about changes that are necessary for the organization; employees on lower levels, on the other hand, react with irrational and emotional fear and resist all types of change (for a critical analysis, see Dent and Galloway Goldberg, 1999). I have a small suggestion for the advocates of this perspective: bring about an organizational change that includes halving the working time and doubling the wages of the employees – then measure their reactions. My hypothesis is that you will not be able to register an awful lot of irrational fear and resistance regarding that change. Incidentally, a famous experiment of this kind has, in fact, been carried out, although I have not seen it mentioned in any discussions about 'resistance to change': in 1914, Henry Ford raised his workers' wages from $2.34 to $5.00 a day, while at the same time cutting their working day to eight hours. No anguish or fear could be noted among those workers; on the contrary, he succeeded in counteracting both unionization and the enormous amount of labour turnover at the plant. Resistance has more to do with the content of the change than with the change per se. Further, the reactions are usually quite rational – not to mention intentional and creative – which we will see in the following narratives. Resistance is, furthermore, also present when there is no change. All in all, resistance and organizational misbehaviour are due to other reasons than change itself.

Other strongly value-laden approaches are used when researching organizational misbehaviour by employees. All misbehaviour can, for example, be called a dysfunctional act, since it is not functional as far as employers are concerned. It can even be called sabotage because everything that employees do to counteract the goals of the organization sabotages these. It is obvious that researchers, too, manoeuvre through the contradictions and dilemmas of working life. So do I, of course. In this book, I take the view that organizational misbehaviour by employees is not based on a general fear of change, that it is not always dysfunctional as regards the goals of the organization, and that not all misbehaviour is sabotage. Instead, organizational misbehaviour is based on people striving for dignity at work when this is threatened by their working conditions. Naturally, it can be said that taking one's point of departure in the dignity of working people is equally value-laden, although there are good moral and philosophical arguments that it is a more reasonable standpoint (Sayer, 2007a). I have no problem with that.

The theme of this book is organizational misbehaviour during struggles regarding the frontier of control in the contested terrain of the workplace, with the manoeuvring in the contradictions and dilemmas being seen from the perspective of the employees. This does not mean that they reflect a simple contradiction between managers and operatives. Managers do not always enjoy dignity at work and they do not always threaten the dignity of their subordinates. Management is not homogeneous; on the contrary, there are many conflicts and fights between managers on different levels and in different professions – for example, between production engineers and human relations managers (Major and Hopper, 2005). Moreover, middle managers often find themselves in a very difficult situation as they can be criticized both from above and from below (Fenton-O'Creevy, 1998).

Much of the resistance literature has neglected management misbehaviour, mainly studying management control versus worker resistance. However, there is a control hierarchy within management as well, thus organizational misbehaviour occurs, of course, in these higher echelons of the workplace: there are also frontiers of control within management, with that terrain being contested too. The result is that there is resistance not only between management on the one hand and operatives on the other, but also within the hierarchy of managers. Thus I am also saying that resistance is a hierarchical phenomenon. Resistance is directed upwards within a power hierarchy. In the literature there are a good number of typologies of resistance and organizational misbehaviour (e.g. Ackroyd and Thompson, 1999; Bélanger and Thuderoz, 2010; Hodson, 1991; Prasad and Prasad, 1998), which build on different definitions of what this is all about. For the time being, my definition of organizational misbehaviour will be 'everything that employees do or think that their superiors do not want them to do or think'. In Part III, I delve deeper into this definition when presenting a new model for analysing employees' (workers' as well as managers') ways of counteracting threats against their dignity.

The narratives

Following this introduction, there are a number of narratives about organizational misbehaviour. Except for the first and last, these have been gathered from social science articles and books. However, I peel away much of the theoretical argument and just relate the stories (which does not mean, of course, that they are 'theory-free', whatever that might connote). These narratives come from many different countries, industries, occupations and workplaces, but nothing can be generalized to working life per se. Each narrative is only what it is.

Most of them play out in the United Kingdom or the United States, but there are also stories from countries such as Sweden and Norway, Australia and Ireland, China and Malaysia, Italy and France. Many types of workplace are involved, such as pulp and paper mills, railway companies, night clubs, shops, aquatic centres, aeroplanes, hotels, restaurants, blinds factories, bakeries, universities and casinos. Most of these can be found in the private sector, but a few of them are in the public sector. We will also encounter quite a few occupations. Among them are factory workers and exotic dancers, printers and web designers, operators and maids working in private homes, plant managers, hotel managers, middle managers and supervisors, cocktail waitresses, barmaids and blackjack dealers, flight attendants and university professors. If you feel that narratives are lacking from one particular area – the public sector, for example – this shortage may simply be due to my not having been able to find enough social science studies suitable for conversion into stories about that particular area.

After the narratives there are two concluding chapters where I suggest a terminology aimed at helping the analysis of organizational misbehaviour. I position this discussion last in the book because I do not want the narratives to be analysed as part of the initial reading. If you want to analyse them later, feel free to do so, but please start by enjoying them merely as stories.

Part II
The Narrative About

Resistance frequently contains elements of consent and consent often incorporates aspects of resistance.

(Collinson, 1994: 60)

2
The Staircase

An ergonomist studied the spatial design of a factory.

'What do you think about the premises here?' he asked a worker during an interview.

'Fantastic, brilliant!' he answered.

'Well,' the ergonomist said, a bit surprised by this enthusiasm, 'is there anything special that you're thinking about?'

'You see, behind that door there is a staircase and behind the staircase is a space that no foreman has ever noticed. There I have a mattress to take a nap on when I can get away. So these premises are very good.'

3
The Strippers' Music

At this 'exotic dance club' the strippers, or 'exotic dancers', were not paid by the owner. Instead, they had to pay both him and a disk jockey a fee, and part of their duties also included selling at least ten drinks per night. Their only income was the money they were able to induce their customers to give them. It was thus important for the strippers to have regular and generous customers in order to at least earn a more or less secure wage.

Originally, the dancers could choose the music that was played while they performed, but one day the owner said: 'This is a classy place and our customers don't want to hear rap, hip-hop or heavy metal.' The only music that could be played was from the Top 40. Anyone breaking the rule would be fined $20.00. The owner was not just afraid that the club's clientele of white middle-class men would be scared off by other kinds of music, losing him customers and thus profit, he also disliked some of the exotic dancers' choice of music because they liked songs that protested against white middle-class culture. That music was a repudiation of what the club stood for. However, it helped the exotic dancers to get on. It expressed what they were unable to express themselves. It said 'go to hell!' to the owner and the customers alike.

In the dressing room, more and more often the dancers discussed what could be done about it. 'We should all play what we want,' they said. 'Without us, who is going to come into this place?' They started to tip the DJs extra to play their forbidden music and then paid the owner the fines. But they also rallied their regulars to resist the new rule. The strippers told their regulars to ask for the music they wanted played. For example, one of them told one of her regulars that this song was *our* song – it's your song and mine, but I'm not allowed to play it. On hearing this, the customer went to the manager and demanded that the song be played while she performed. And, as the customer is always right, the manager was unable to refuse. The request for dangerous and inferior music did not come from an exotic dancer but from a customer. After a few weeks, the owner gave up and the dancers were once again able to choose their own music.

The punters were still their only source of income, and they still had to pay fees to both the owner and the DJs, but they had at least recaptured some small measure of control over their jobs: the music.

(Egan, 2006)

4
The Recalcitrant Factory Workers

A leading plant in the world in its industry, part of a national group and having been making great profits for a long period of time, had 90 per cent of the market share when it was acquired by a gigantic US-owned group. Before the takeover, an informally negotiated, flexible work organization had evolved. Management, workers and the union had quietly reached agreement on how work was to be carried out. This meant that, in practice, the workers themselves were running most things and they were free to take great liberties; for example, bunking off during their shifts without anyone complaining. At the same time, they worked really hard when necessary. If a product was defective, they immediately corrected the fault. If a delivery date was risking an overrun, they made massive efforts to meet the deadline. But, when the workers reached the informally agreed quota, they did other things. These included playing cards, chess or darts, arranging table tennis tournaments, taking naps and going to a nearby pub.

Following acquisition, the new group strongly demanded changes to the work organization because of stiffer competition and threatened profitability. Productivity had to be improved and profits maintained. The thinking behind the new way of working was strengthening management control, which was regarded as a prerequisite for reducing costs, improving quality and raising productivity. Two of the features were the introduction of a new type of team and *kaizen*, which is the constant improvement of productivity and efficiency. The workers' flexibility was to be replaced by a flexibility planned by management and initiated from above.

All these management measures were met with suspicion and resistance on the part of the workers. The new foremen and middle managers, who had been recruited from the shop floor, were constantly reminded of their old sins. One of them was called Disco Dave, because he used to make frequent visits to a nearby club while on night shift. Now, every time he tried to make the workers do things they did not like, he was told 'not to make a song and dance about things'. Another manager had constructed a cardboard nest in which he used to take naps. Now, when he complained about the night shift's poor performance, he was told, 'it's hard working nights', and 'people who live in cardboard houses shouldn't throw stones'. The new managers were constantly facing questions, such as how they had the nerve or the barefaced cheek to talk about flexibility or team working without laughing themselves.

Management maintained that the workers were unreasonable, unrealistic and afraid of change. The workers' response was that the new way of working was 'bullshit' and that it was a 'con' for management to take over control of the work by spying on the workers via all the reports that were to be delivered. They suggested that managers should try working on the shop floor to have the experience of 'staying up all night' and to be told by 'bullshitters who did fuck all' that greater productivity was necessary. The idea was rejected initially, but then a new senior manager thought that it would perhaps be 'a valuable experience' for the production managers. In doing so, they could also demonstrate their commitment to the changes and their support for the company's corporate culture, centred on a 'search for continuous improvement' by 'working together to win'. The workers interpreted this culture as another attempt to manipulate their thoughts and to 'get inside their heads'. The manager responsible for arranging this valuable experience had no success. The only concrete advice he got was that the experiment should last at least five years if it was to result in any experience to speak of. The new senior manager changed his mind and nothing came of the suggestion.

After this failure, management came up with the idea of initiating a number of pilot projects in the sections that it considered to be reasonably accommodating. Change teams were introduced with the intention of spreading this new way of working according to the principle of example being better than precept. In this way, the workers would let go of their fear of change and realize that the new way was not about working harder but working smarter. When this strategy failed, management instead concentrated on the sections that were regarded to be the most militant ones. 'If we can make them change, then everyone else will change' was the idea. Change agents were recruited from the shop floor, but this experiment also fell on stony ground.

Finally, one of the senior managers who had been sent from the US to end the problems and implement the new way of working sighed: 'Coming here has been a nightmare and a fuckin' career disaster.' The plant was, in his view, one of the most militant he had ever seen. Furthermore, it was not the union that was militant but the workers who wanted to maintain their own kind of flexibility. Moreover, if the plant remains in existence, they will probably continue doing so.

(Ezzamel, Willmot and Worthington, 2001, 2004)

5
The Satisfied Department

When Establishment Printers won a contract for a government Department, senior management decided to introduce a new work-flow/information management system. There were two reasons for this. The first was that it would help to achieve production targets. The second related to providing detailed invoices automatically generated by the information system – the Department did not trust the documentation produced by the workers and wanted objective data from the system.

Work at Establishment Printers could not be planned long-term. Sometimes there were jobs that had to be done immediately and that therefore had to jump the queue, printed matter volumes varied markedly and machines did not run properly, resulting in delayed jobs. The occupational groups that were directly involved – machine operators, administrative staff and shop-floor managers – cooperated on several strategies in order to make work run smoothly and efficiently, in spite of these problems. All the machine operators received their orders on a form from the administrators and they were supposed to do these jobs in the order in which they arrived in their in-trays. However, the operators resorted the jobs according to their own assessment of how complicated and time-consuming they were. In that way, the machines were utilized in the most efficient way and work flowed well. Often, they also searched the desks of administrative staff for notes about jobs that had not yet been formally registered. If possible, they printed them off before they were registered, and the administrators cooperated in this procedure.

All the operators were responsible for their own printing machines, but they also monitored each other's work. If one of them had a problem, the others would help out. Furthermore, if an operator was unable to finish a job on time, the others would take it on, incorporate it into their own work and then pass it back. Formally, it looked as if the first machine operator had done the job, but in practice another operator had done it. But it had been done.

It was into this setting of cooperation, which was making work at Establishment Printers flow, that the new information and management system was introduced. The system was described thus:

> It works by organising a work flow for jobs which is based upon a sequential model of the production process. This requires that new jobs first be entered into the system by one of the administrative staff at a PC terminal. A job-number is assigned which the system subsequently uses to recognize the job. When all of the job requests for the day are entered into the system they are allocated to individual printers who begin work on them by entering the job-number on a shop-floor terminal to call up the job from the system. Operators are also required to enter their own identity numbers and the process they are about to initiate. Operators also enter the number of copies, the type and colour of the paper and, during the course of printing, the number of wasted copies and the duration of any down-time. Once operators have completed their work on jobs, they enter this information followed by the initiation of any other process that they have to undertake. When they have finished all of their designated work on a job they log off and turn the job over either to other operators or to the dispatcher, as specified on the job-ticket. These staff, in turn, go through the logging in and logging off procedures. In these ways [the system] is intended automatically to organize a smooth flow of work across the print room floor and to gather data about the processes a job goes through. (55–6)

However, things did not turn out exactly as senior management and the Department had expected. For both the administrative staff and the machine operators, it turned out that there was quite a lot of extra work due to the repeated occasions of logging in and out. This did not matter so much on big jobs, but on small ones – for example, printing only a couple of pages – this took up a considerable chunk of the job time. The system further required that only one operator could be logged onto a job at a time, rendering impossible much of the flexibility that had been created by running two jobs simultaneously. Moreover, it was no longer possible to start a job before it was logged onto the system. Finally, the system was based on the principle that individual operators performed the various steps of the labour process. Each operator had an individual identification number and the system connected this to the job identification number. This prevented operators from assuming collective responsibility for smoothing the workflow.

The machine operators, the administrative staff and the shop-floor managers were not very enthusiastic over the fact that the control they had once had over the labour process had now been built into the new information and management system. This control had previously ensured that work could be performed in a smooth and efficient way. If they were to achieve that goal again, they would have to regain their influence over the work process – their autonomy. Gradually, the three occupational groups jointly found ways of achieving that goal. In practice, they closed down the system for parts of the working day and then fed it with the information that was needed for the invoices to be sent to the Department. It was done as follows. The administrators entered the jobs into the system at the beginning of the working day, but then it was not used further that day. The operators did not log onto the shop-floor terminals but instead documented the jobs on paper in the same way they had been doing before the system had been introduced. At the end of the day, they delivered the information to the administrative staff, who programmed the system with data the next morning in a way that made it look as if the system itself had generated the data the day before. The Department then received the detailed invoices it wanted, showing every sign of being based on the workflow/information management system's objective data.

The machine operators, the administrative staff and the shop-floor managers did not try to fool the Department or senior management. True, the data the Department received was not the system's objective data but the operators' subjective data. This was, however, merely a consequence of the efforts of the employees at Establishment Printers to regain control of their work, and thus the flow and efficiency of the work process. Senior management was ignorant of what was going on and the Department was very satisfied with Establishment Printers as it always met its delivery dates and documented its invoices so well.

(Button, Mason and Sharrock, 2003)

6
Fair Exchange in Milanese Shops

Employees sometimes see their jobs as an exchange with their employer. That is also what workers at big retail companies in Milan did. They regarded the relationship between themselves and their employers as a fair exchange – or at least that is what they thought it should be. The relationship ought to be one of equal rights and duties. If they provided work effort and a responsible attitude, then they would expect a decent wage and satisfactory working conditions in return. An important part of the latter was stable employment and working hours. If the employer did not live up to the conditions of this exchange but departed from the norms of justice, the employees would take it as an expression of disrespect for them as human beings.

The retail company employers did break the norms: they did not follow the rules of fair exchange, nor did they keep their part of the bargain. They wanted flexibility, and the way for them to achieve it was to make the workers become flexible. This was accomplished by using part-time and temporary employment, overtime at short notice and spontaneous shift changes. It was a culture of 'forced availability' through which working conditions became the result of day-to-day bargaining between supervisors and individual employees. If someone refused to work overtime on a specific occasion, it would take some time before they were asked again. Most of the workers wanted overtime as the wages were so low. Instead of fair exchange, the workers had to constantly seek individual 'favours' from supervisors. They did not get the stability they wanted; instead, the flexibility they provided the employer with resulted in instability in their own lives.

They interpreted the precarisation they felt as an expression of disrespect by the employers. The exchange was not fair, so why should they be fair? The employers were not following the rules of exchange, so why should they? One of the workers explained: 'If management thinks that people are machines, and working conditions are just bad, of course, I'll be less productive, as a consequence. At the moment that's exactly how things are.'

One of their reactions was to distance themselves from the exchange and instead start looking at their relationship with their employers as a game to be played and an opportunity to further their own individual interests. One employee told us, for example, how he acts during performance appraisals, which the employer intended to be a participatory event:

> Yes, it's a duty to participate [in regular one-on-one interviews used for performance appraisal]. I talk a lot [in these interviews]. I write a lot of things in their questionnaires, too, a lot of things I don't believe in. But, they want to hear these things and I just play the game. I don't know if the managers see it the same way, as a game. But I don't care, at least for two hours I don't work: I simply talk, talk, and that guy listens, I talk and talk. And, look, I do have my questions, too: 'You want to know about me, so I also want to know about you' [...] Everybody just talks nonsense in these interviews, everything they want to hear; but then we also use the time to talk about other things, [...] things we don't like about the work, that should be changed. (2009: 94)

Other types of resistance also occurred, such as working more slowly in order to create extra time to have a chat, and taking longer breaks than allowed. Furthermore, the employees held back their creativity, their enthusiasm and their emotional investment in the job. The employers did not create a fair exchange through decent wages and acceptable working conditions, thus the employees did not provide them with a full work effort and a responsible attitude.

(Carls, 2007, 2009)

7
The Disappointed Associates

Japanese factories began establishing themselves in regions with high unemployment in the United States. They were seeking to transplant Japanese work organization principles. The car manufacturer Subaru-Isuzu Automotive (SIA) established a factory close to Lafayette in Indiana. Trade unions were banned – the company and the employees were going to be like one big family and the unions were portrayed as the equivalent of someone who comes between a man and his wife.

Many people were looking for a job, so the company could pick and choose. All job-seekers had to be screened, including their reflections on these questions before even being considered for employment at SIA:

> Am I committed to the concept of 'Quality Consciousness'? Am I willing to share my ideas with others and to constantly strive to improve in all areas? Am I ready to work in a fast-pace work environment? Can I work with others in a team? (1995: 20)

Being classified as a 'team player' was the most important result of the screening process. However, many applicants were able to see through the tests, and once they had got their jobs they thought they had succeeded in manipulating the tests rather than actually meeting these requirements – something that especially applied to their views on management. About his strategy, one of them said: 'I wanted the job and I was not going to blow my chances by really letting the company know how I felt.'

Once employed, they were not called employees but, in company terminology, 'Associates'. However, the associates were not quite ready to begin working in production. First, they had to undergo a period of training. To their surprise, the technical skills to cope with the job only accounted for a small part of that training. Learning the company culture, which was said to build on reciprocal trust and was aimed at beating competitors, seemed to be more important. SIA was unique, the Associates were taught, in that everybody is equal, all voices are heard and safety is always in focus.

The Associates were expected to be prepared to always conform to company requirements. For example, a passage from the *Associate Handbook* states:

> Involve yourself enthusiastically. We are not asking Associates to work without compensation, but we do ask that all of us help establish a workplace where creativity comes naturally. It is natural to cooperate with each other as a team, trying to eliminate all possible waste, looking for ways to improve, and keeping each one's own work area a clean, happy place. After all, work is the place where many of us spend an entire third of our 24-hour day, and fully half of our waking hours.
>
> When people work only to get paid, their workplace becomes very uninteresting. When they participate in an organization with enthusiasm, however, the very same workplace will prove an interesting, even exciting, place for them to be. (1995: 95)

When the Associates started on real production work, they soon became aware that all the talk about open communication and respect for everyone's views did not count for much in practice. Or, as a group leader said, when two of them complained about being put on a different shift from the one they were promised: 'The company only takes input from Associates on subjects the company chooses.' It became ever clearer that Associates' suggestions and wishes were simply being ignored, especially when it came to questions about the speed of the line, overtime and the staffing arrangements for the shifts. The participation of the Associates turned out to be restricted to improving quality.

The worst thing that could happen to a worker was for them to fall behind. This had nothing to do with the loss of productivity, but with work becoming chaotic and even more stressful than normal. However, the work was planned in such a way that the teams had to balance the whole time on the brink of falling behind. Part of this involved each team having its own piece of music. If somebody fell behind, they had to pull a cord hanging over the line at each station, which caused that team's music to be played over the PA system – and it continued to be played until they had solved the problem and the team leader had marked this by pulling the cord again. All this was monitored by a computer, but it entailed, of course, extra pressure, in that it was broadcast that the team could not keep up. All the positive management talk was soon overtaken by the reality of the line, its speed gradually being increased. Opportunities to joke, play and socialize during work were steadily squeezed out. During training, there was much talk of the importance of a safe workplace, but along with the increased stress came more and more accidents. Nothing was done, however, to change the way the work was organized to overcome the injuries. Instead, it turned out that every Associate was individually responsible for not having an accident. It was, according to management practice, an individual problem, not a question of work organization.

Against the backdrop of the Associates' disappointment over management not living up to the promises made during training, many forms of resistance appeared. For example, the working day started with each team performing a decreed ritual, which was akin to what an ice hockey team does in front of its goalkeeper before a game is about to start. The team gathered in a circle and each Associate stretched an arm into the centre. The team leader appointed an Associate who had to say something inspiring ahead of that day's work. However, most of these messages consisted of jokes rather than something intended to raise productivity or create loyalty towards the company. For example, the Associate in question might say, in the kind of exaggeratedly deep voice found in TV commercials: 'I'm proud to be an American.' After this, everyone had to bring their other arm into the ring and shout 'Yosh!' All the teams were instructed to do this, but no one was quite clear about what 'yosh' meant. Most Associates thought, however, that it meant something like 'Let's go!'

More collective types of resistance also grew. One example relates to the line initially being stopped five minutes before the down-tools signal. The reason for this was that the Associates were given time to put away their tools and clean up their stations in order to get themselves organized for the next working day. But then management decided – without consulting any of the Associates – that the line would run right up to the signal. The Associates were then expected to do the necessary tidying up after their working day had finished. All the Associates got very upset when the decision was put before them at team meetings, as it was contrary to everything they had been told about company policy, which included exerting an influence on decisions and getting paid for all their work. In spite of the resistance shown at the meetings, the line was run right up to the signal. From that day on, all the Associates let go of what they were doing when they heard the signal and went home, so the team leader had to do the cleaning up for the whole team.

A final example: management decided to introduce a second shift. The Associates then had to rotate between the shifts. The problems that this rotation caused in their private lives, due to ever-changing working hours, were totally disregarded. Quietly, the Associates built up an informal network, which covered the whole workplace, in order to militate against rotation. They agreed that they would argue against shift rotation at all meetings. The daily team, department and plant meetings were suddenly dominated by complaints and criticisms regarding the decision to introduce shift rotation. The inconsistency of that decision with regard to the company's official philosophy was pointed out constantly – management was not complying with its own philosophy. One day, at team meetings, the Associates were notified right across the workplace that there would not be any more shift rotation.

(Graham, 1993, 1995)

8
The Employees Who Were Not on Brand

All were agreed, from the executives to the employees on the floor: The enormous drive for a corporate cultural framework, Brand Essence, was a failure. The only question was: Who was to blame?

The company had recently made a large number of employees redundant and was in the middle of outsourcing and cost-cutting programmes. At the same time, it needed those employees who were left to use all their knowledge and creativity to increase profit. The executives and the human resources (HR) department decided to launch a cultural programme aimed at making the employees align themselves with company goals, whereby a number of behavioural characteristics were pointed out as essential in order for the company to become a winner. These characteristics were called Brand Essence, and this was said to consist of 'passionate, reliable and innovative' employees. The new culture was propagated around the workplace, at training sessions and workshops, and in brochures and DVDs. All this material was full of terms such as 'warmth, humanity, empathy, integrity, life's journey, best in class, challenging, inspiring, creative and optimistic'. The employees were supposed to 'live the essence', as well as talk it, write it and express it in their body language. Using the company's term, all employees had to be 'on brand'.

But employee resistance to this branding was so strong that the whole programme collapsed. Staff refused to be on brand for two reasons. First, there was such a gigantic gap between the rhetoric of the new culture and the reality of company policies regarding redundancy and cost-cutting that they felt cheated – they regarded the cultural messages as deceptive. One of them said: 'It's very hard to swallow, extremely hard, they're telling you one day how important you are to them and the next day they're making more redundant. [...] It's just hypocrisy after hypocrisy; they don't eat their own dog food basically.' Secondly, the employees opposed being told how to think and act by the HR department:

> For professionals like me or relatively intelligent people it really is insulting [...] massively negative, it's like 'where is my school uniform?' when I'm getting up in the morning. I'm a professional you know, I've been to college and I've done all these things and I've qualified and you know there's people even more qualified than me and they're suffering this. (110)

It was obvious to the employees that the managers and executives themselves were not living up to the standards of warmth, humanity and empathy enshrined in Brand Essence.

The executives blamed the failure of the cultural programme on the way it was implemented by the HR department and junior managers. They could not see anything wrong with Brand Essence itself, only in the manner it was being implemented. The HR managers felt the same way, except that they were not to be blamed – they had done all they could, they thought – but the junior managers had made mistakes during implementation. The junior managers, who were supposed to spread the message directly to the work teams, realized that there would be major difficulties convincing the employees of the blessings of Brand Essence. They saw it as their duty to try, but they understood that the new culture would be regarded as hypocrisy. They blamed the HR people and the executives for not understanding the realities of the shop floor. And we know what the employees thought: it was all an insult to their dignity as professionals and adults, as well as being a hypocritical rhetoric far from company reality as they knew it.

(Cushen, 2009)

9
Careful Carelessness

Coffee cups and cans of soft drinks often stood right beside keyboards and someone could easily have knocked them over. People forgot to shut down their computers at night, and to save important documents. Information ended up in the wrong place. During conversations between managers, the conviction took root that this was not simply a matter of accidents or negligence, but systematic and deliberate resistance on the part of the employees. One of the managers invented a term for what was going on – 'careful carelessness' – and this soon spread throughout the workplace.

Nobody was punished as nothing could be proved. Actually, only the employees knew whether or not the careful carelessness really existed, or whether it was just a figment of management's imagination – and they are keeping quiet.

(P. Prasad and A. Prasad, 2000; A. Prasad and P. Prasad, 2001)

10
The Teams That Drifted Apart

The plant was newly built and, when production started, team organization was introduced in order to foster a feeling of commitment to work and to make the employees identify with the company. The team concept, with its emphasis on community and influence, was to permeate the entire workplace. There were to be teams on two levels within the organization. One was directly related to production, entailing that each shift was to be a united and integrated group. Independently of occupation and tasks, the employees were to cooperate and help each other to achieve productivity goals. The teams were even provided with a small budget to arrange common leisure activities. On this basis, a strong sense of social solidarity developed within the production teams.

The second level on which the idea of teamwork was to be applied was the company as a whole: all of us, management and workers, are members of the same team. We have common interests and shared goals, and we work together in order to achieve them. The notion of the company as a big, joint team was propagated on posters all over the workplace.

At the beginning, things worked out as planned. Productivity was high and loyalty grew in the production teams as well as in the company team. Soon, however, the two types of team began to drift apart. In many matters, management actions ran foul of the talk about common interests, worker autonomy and control. Strengthened by the solidarity within the production teams, the workers started to dissociate themselves from the loyalty within the company team. More and more, they made their own choice regarding which norms to follow – and that choice was their very own norms within the production teams rather than the ones prescribed from above by the company team. In company surveys, managers were clearly able to read how trust in them had been dropping steadily. The production teams were intended as instruments of management's control of the workers, but instead they had become an obstacle to this control. A senior manager complained that the workers 'have this feeling of being in it together, as if they are a family. So they just look to protect one another instead of doing what they need to do!' It was the company team that was supposed to be like a big family, but now the production teams had become families that were in opposition to the company team.

In order to counteract this development, management arranged a 'Refresher Course' for all employees. Everybody went away together for a whole day and engaged in group exercises to learn about communal interests, which included the fact that managers and workers literally had to hold hands. This only resulted in increasing the workers' cynicism with regard to the way management was using its budget.

Management's next step was to announce a reorganization of the production teams. The composition of all the teams was to be changed and the employees moved around. In this way – according to the plan – the solidarity between the team members would be broken and loyalty to the company team would be re-established. The workers realized that this was the intention and would entail stronger management control over important parts of their work. A representative of each team met in a special group in order to discuss countermeasures. The group wrote a protest letter in which they argued that the new organization would make the working environment worse and increase the risk of accidents. It was also, to quote the letter, a deceit to the entire team concept. It was an expression of what the employees had been suspecting for some time, namely that management had started to make decisions above their heads. Where was the communal interest and worker influence?

The letter was distributed all over the factory. A couple of days later, a petition was circulated, signed by all the workers but one, which once again confirmed the resistance to the plans for a reorganization. It was also sent to company headquarters. Finally, management was forced to give up its plans and the production teams survived. The workers had managed to turn the production teams against the company team and had used management rhetoric about participation and autonomy as a lever to gain a certain amount of control over their working conditions.

(Vallas, 2003)

11
Two Aquatic Centres

Both aquatic centres have the same purpose: offering people a chance to cool off and have a refreshing bath, to paying customers in order to make a profit. They are, consequently, in the same market, but they differ very much in their treatment of their employees and, in doing so, in the amount of resistance and organizational misbehaviour they encounter.

At one of them, the owner works with his employees. When it is raining or when there are few or no bathers for other reasons, he encourages the employees simply to relax or study. He shows that this is okay by sitting down and reading. In return, he can trust his employees to work hard and take care of his customers when the place is crowded. At such times, the workers do not try to get out of doing their work – quite the reverse. New employees trying to do this are admonished by their fellow workers:

> We did have one girl who'd just park her arse on the counter and we really hated people sitting on the counter, but she'd just sit there and you'd say 'how 'bout you do such "n" such' and she'd be like, just not interested. She just wanted to sit around and do nothing and that pissed other people off. She wasn't made to feel very welcome, nobody would talk to her and we'd give her shitty jobs...so she didn't hang around that long. (51)

Labour turnover is relatively low, as are absences, and resistance and organizational misbehaviour are almost unknown.

The other aquatic centre is family owned, with seven family members making up the board of directors. They seldom agree on anything, resulting in managers receiving strongly formulated, but contradictory, orders from the owners. They are never satisfied with anything and always demand that the staff work harder, independently of the flow of customers. One of the managers expresses his feelings towards the board in this way:

> It really makes you bitter, though, you know, to be put in this position of responsibility but not be given any positive responsibility or encouragement. I might as well have been scrubbing the shithouses for all the respect I was given.... I guess the only way a lot of these managers knew how to protect themselves was to adopt sort of guerrilla tactics. You know, screw them before they screw you. (54–5)

All in all, the owners' way of acting has resulted in not only the workers but also the managers talking about themselves as 'us', and about the owners as 'them'. Everybody resists the owners' orders and there is misbehaviour regarding their rules.

They all withhold their labour as much as they can. The managers take three-hour lunch breaks, claiming that they are holding important meetings, while the workers also dodge work whenever they get the chance. Management even shuns all orders by the board to discipline the workers. One of them explains: 'If the managers are doing what they can to get out of their own work, what could you legitimately do to stop the staff from doing it? Besides, what motivation was there to try?' Management and workers both steal as much as they think they can get away with from the firm – the managers more, of course, as they have greater opportunities.

The first aquatic centre or the second – which one do you think makes more profit?

(Townsend, 2004)

12
Peer Review in the Factory of the Future

When the big combine was subjected to severe competition in the 1980s, management decided to change the organization from one of mass-production and managerial hierarchy to a flexibile and innovative one with higher quality in production. In order to mark the occasion, an entirely new plant was being built. It was called the 'Factory of the Future'. Trade unions were forbidden (they were regarded as an unwanted external influence), teams were introduced, the employees were to be empowered and managers would no longer have authority simply because of their position but would function as technical coaches. The road to the plant was constructed in such a way that it was physically impossible to carry out demonstrations or arrange meetings outside. All employees were carefully screened so that anyone who could bring suspicious attitudes and values into the factory could be sifted out. The job interviews therefore contained a detailed mapping of the applicant's mentality and social life. The HR department saw to it that only one member of a family was employed, that people who already had friends there friends were not hired and that only a small number from the local area got work. Management did not want the employees to share any other allegiances than the team and the company. Management even went to such lengths as to forbid newspapers at the workplace, because that kind of external information could disturb the concentration on the team, the work tasks and production. Management also tried to impose a strong company culture in a reign supreme in order to colonize the consciousness of the employees – or as one of the employees commented: 'Basically they are trying to change your personality.' The extent to which this was achieved was measured in surveys.

An important part of the organization of the Factory of the Future was the process of peer review, which was to be conducted entirely within the teams and by the employees themselves. It meant that workers were to judge their own behaviour and attitudes in many respects, laid down by management. Among these parameters were individual efficiency in work, development of new skills and quality consciousness, but also behaviour according to team and company culture. The team held a monthly meeting, during which the workers studied graphs of the points each team member had got and then three workers were selected to be commented on by all other workers. None of the three was allowed to speak until the others had made their criticism and given their scores. In this way, any deviation from management norms could be detected at an early stage and the workers were to discipline themselves. The team's results were reported to a central database, through which management could have full control over the whole workforce. Teams with low scores had further training in the peer-review process or team-building exercises. The peer review was a collective process, instilled to strengthen the individual's regulation of him- or herself. An essential element of the adaptation to the more intense competition was to adjust the consciousness of the employees to organizational demands of the Factory of the Future.

Can there be any resistance under such working conditions? Management seemed to have closed all possibilities. Initially, no misbehaviour could be detected – teamwork and autonomy were appreciated by the workers. But gradually the idea was spread within more and more teams that they were being manipulated. Teams and peer reviews were no longer regarded as expressions of autonomy and self-control, but as a new way for management to command and control the work. It felt more and more strange and embarrassing to pass judgement on fellow workers. Often the peer-review meetings were cancelled with the excuse that production required the workers' time. Quietly the mean results were spread among the teams and were then adjusted in such a way that the differences became minimal. Thereby the computer system could no longer perceive the result of single teams. At those meetings that were held, there was no more criticism – everyone agreed with everyone else about everything. The meetings now seldom functioned as law courts; instead, the workers who stuck out were those who still followed the instructions from management for peer-review meetings. Most workers started to follow newly formed, collective norms. And those not following those norms were sanctioned. A worker who had recently changed from a team that still carried out peer review according to management instructions to a team that did not said:

> If you come in and start giving people 2s, which is saying that there's room for improvement, people will stop talking to you. So you change and start giving people higher scores. The minimum you give is a 3. (1998: 187)

The self-organization among workers had recaptured them from the company culture of the Factory of the Future.

(McKinlay and Taylor, 1996, 1998)

13
The Maids Who Did Not Want to Be Maids

Almost everywhere, maids, domestics and other occupational groups working in private homes come from low positions in class and ethnic hierarchies. This story is about Afro-American women working in the homes of white people in Kentucky. These women are very experienced at their jobs, as they have worked this way for many years. That is also one reason why they have been able to develop strategies to establish a certain autonomy and dignity at work in spite of their socially subordinate positions. Something that has contributed towards making it easier for them is the fact that they have benefited from a rather good labour market while there have also been other jobs available to them as black working-class women. Furthermore, they have often had to do two or three jobs at the same time. Thus, if they were to quit one of these in protest, it would not mean economic disaster.

They have also had good role models in friends and relatives – mothers, grandmothers, mothers-in-law, aunts – who have, or have had, the same type of work. They have always heard stories about how to handle employers and others in private homes. For example, an aunt told one of them the following tale. The daughter of the white family let everything drop where she stood, her clothes were all over the place – bras, stockings, dresses, evening gowns, clean and dirty garments mixed indiscriminately. In vain, the aunt asked her to keep her things in better order as she had no way of knowing what was to be washed and what was to be hung up in the closets. Finally, she got tired of the problems that the daughter was causing and took all her party clothes and put them in the laundry basket. When the girl asked for a ball gown, the aunt answered that she had put it in the dirty laundry with everything else she had found on the floor. After that, the girl stopped throwing her clothes around. What this story tells others working in private homes is, of course, you have to train your employers in order to make your job easier.

The white women, who are the actual employers, hire the black women to get away from (some of) their domestic work. Therefore, they want to get as much work as possible out of this labour power. It is thus in their interest that domestic work is regarded as easy to perform and that it does not require any skills. By virtue of that, the wages can be kept low, too. From the perspective of the Afro-American women, it is important instead to emphasize that this type of work requires a lot of knowledge and experience – and also that different parts of the work require different types of skill. The employers want a single occupation, 'maid', with low status and low wages. The black women resist this and try to make it a practice that it is a whole set of different occupations with varying (and high) skill requirements. In that way, they can also obstruct more and more tasks of different kinds from becoming defined as part of their job.

With the strength of a dignified occupation that has specific skills, these employees can maintain autonomy at work, some of them in a clandestine way: 'I've had them to tell me would you clean such and such, don't use this and don't use that, and I listen. And when they leave I clean it my way. Yeah, I know what works for me. I take their instructions, but I do it my way.' Others defend their autonomy more explicitly, like this cook:

> I do not have anybody to dictate to me. And if you are going to dictate to me, I don't need the job. That's the way I feel about it. Because I know what I'm doing. Now, they may ask you to make something extra, that's okay, but you don't come into your kitchen, I don't care if it is your kitchen because it is mine while I'm there. You don't come in there and tell me what to do. (220)

Their employers, and perhaps middle- and upper-class people more generally, may regard the work that domestics do as of low value, both in terms of status and wage. The workers try to resist and maintain dignified occupational specializations with autonomy for the 'maids'.

(Kousha, 1994)

14
Responsible Co-Workers and Irresponsible Counter-Workers

The Railway Authority was to be deregularized and marketized. The state grants were to be strongly diminished and the authority had to procure other receipts. At the same time there was still no other customer than the administrative parts of the same authority. But new and buyer–seller-oriented organizational forms, adjusted to a market, were to be introduced. 'We must be more modern', management thought, and thereby they meant that the organization should be more like a market agent: the public sector is antiquated, now there will be a market! What marked this transformation was the adjustment to the market. This was to make the employees 'move double-quick', as the managers liked to say. Instead of the buyer purchasing services from divisions of the department, they were now to purchase them in competition with 'agents' and 'players' at the market. There were almost only positive associations with the market and almost only negative associations with the public sector: the rigid bureaucratic authority that, protected by its monopoly, could trot along at its own pace totally unencumbered by what happened around it. With the help of the market, this department would now be restructured into an entrepreneurial consultant business. 'The business' was to be put at the centre of the organization; resources were to be used where needed without respect for old borders. Consciousness of the importance of the customer was to permeate the organization. It was all about navigating 'in the jungle' as another common expression said. And efficiency was the key to getting by, especially considering how inefficient work had been in the old monopoly department. Public organizations were by definition inefficient, private ones by definition efficient. The market is inevitable and we have to adjust to it – that was the linchpin of the management perspective. Workers and managers faced the same powers, there were no alternatives, and it was all about keeping up with the development.

Adjustment to the market also required a new type of work organization. The basic idea was that the inefficient, hierarchical and bureaucratic organizations in the public sector had brought about massive negative circumstances for both production and employees. Now a new, borderless and flexible organization had to be created. That meant several things. One was that there should be a core of permanent employees with strong qualifications to perform many different work tasks. This core was to be complemented by casual labour, performing specific tasks at work peaks. Another was that the employees were to be flexible – able to change tasks, departments, offices and geographical placing whenever required to do so. A third issue was that working time was to be entirely adjusted to the work and contract with the customer.

As the customer and the business were to guide everything, all borderlines within the organization were to be broken up; for example, those between occupations and departments. The organization was to be borderless. The former bureaucratic structure with permanent work teams was to be replaced by teams with different competences that were to act as a company within a company. In addition, temporary project groups would be set up to deal with specific contracts.

However, if the borderless organization's adjustment to the inevitable market was to function, a transformation of the employees to responsible co-workers was necessary. In the old day, the protected and secure work in the public sector had created employees characterized by passivity and lack of independence. They had no commercial competence whatsoever; they did not know anything about how to handle customers or the importance of doing business. When managers talked about the workers, they used words like lacking in vision, passive, spoiled, retrogressed, bureaucratic-minded, negative, order executers, dull and stiff – all summarized in the strongly depreciatory term 'civil servant'. Managers often talked about how important it was for the success of the borderless organization on the inevitable market that the label 'civil servant' be removed. Another popular expression was that workers used to the public sector 'hang up their head when they hang up their jacket' when they get to the job.

A specific problem was the workers' great interest in the technical problems of the job. In a way it was, of course, good that the employees engaged in that part of their work, but after all it took energy from what was always the most important issue: interest in business, customers and the economic result. 'The technical knowledge is not to dominate anymore, it is the new technique – business', as one of the managers expressed it. From the managerial perspective, the workers' commitment to solving technical problems in the job meant that they were lacking in vision and passive, because a technical interest meant insufficient interest in business – which was what really mattered. Therefore, management saw as its mission to transform the workers into responsible co-workers, characterized by concentration on the customer and possessing an inherent will to do good business. This was summarized in the expression that the responsible co-worker has a 'comprehensive view', which meant not only directing their energies towards technology and solving specific work tasks but prioritizing a commercial perspective. The personal values of the workers had to be altered in that direction.

The changes were to go from all the negative characteristics of civil servants to 'networking consultants' and 'innovative entrepreneurs'. This would mean that workers would be more responsible, flexible, open, creative, proactive, outgoing, independent, socially competent, positive, able to stand stress and goal-directed. The uniting traits in all these good things were businessmanship and employability. Businessmanship meant that the co-worker should not do any work because it was necessary, only for commercial reasons. Only what was 'billable' through a contract with a customer was to be done. Part of this involved constantly hunting for new contracts, procuring more orders and thus creating an even more profitable business. Employability meant that it was the worker's own responsibility to develop new technical, social and commercial skills in order to be attractive enough to qualify to be part of a project group when a certain contract was finished or on the whole to be attractive for employers.

The workers had a different view, building on their belief that the management perspective was unrealistic. Instead of rejecting the old organization totally, what was positive should be developed. Now management visions were compared to commercial advertisements:

they are not always true and they promise more than they can keep. And the beautiful brochures in which the visions were presented were regarded as somewhat ridiculous: 'It is not that way in reality.'

From this perspective, the talk about the market stands out as rhetoric in defence of the rationalizations that management had carried through, which had resulted in notices to quit and in changes for the worse in working conditions. Earlier the workers had accepted a rather low wage because they regarded it as being in exchange for secure employment. Now security had degraded considerably but the poor wages were still there. If it had been a real market, the wages would have been on a level with those in private enterprises. And: 'All nonsense to and fro about the market! If it had been serious they would have to start with the wages.' There was, however, always money to hire people in the marketing department, to contract consultants and to print advertising folders. If management was as efficient as management in private business was said to be, it should not have met the new market demands with mass notices. Instead it should have used all of its energy to obtain new contracts and new receipts. From this perspective, management hardly acted the way professional managers in a market should act.

The very idea of the inevitable market was contested, especially in relation to security: the new economic approach was a threat towards railroad safety. If workers detected something that was a potential risk, they were no longer allowed to attend to it if it was outside the contract. From the workers' point of view, there was a conflict between the pressure on costs and time on the one hand and security on the other. Their belief was that security must be allowed to cost money and time. Management talked a lot about security, but it tried to build an organization that could not handle security in practice. Instead of all the talk about serving 'the customer', it still ought to be about serving the public through a secure and good product, the way it had always been in the public sector.

In the workers' eyes, the new organization was not flexible and free from boundaries but rather insatiable and insecure. It had been flexible, but in quite another sense than how management suggested. Work used to be flexible with regard to workers being able to come up with their own creative solutions to technical problems. Now it was much more controlled from above and more fragmented. What management really meant by talk about flexibility was a stronger demand on work effort and an intensification of work. Earlier there was an informal agreement that a work order was a recommendation about what should be done and how much time it was to take. If an unexpected problem arose, such as with security, the order could be modified. Now, however, you were only allowed to perform tasks that could be billed – that is not more flexibility but more bureaucracy!

On top of all this came management's demand for a changed personality. This was, the workers thought, an infringement on their private life. Management invested strongly in training campaigns in order to exert an influence on workers' attitudes, but to little effect. One of them said:

> You know, I felt they were trying to brainwash me! It felt like we were in a religious revival meeting, 400 people and a management consultant with three of his disciples and...I can tell you we laughed. But seriously, it was pretty scary and the most frightening thing is that this brainwashing program has used up all the money needed for real training which some of the younger guys really need. (2009: 179)

Management was out of bounds when they insisted on meddling with personal affairs. Workers' personality should not be put under the control of the marketing department.

Further, management's positive talk about engaging in work and participation stood out as new demands – demands that meant that the workers were to break up the division between work and leisure to the advantage of work without any compensation. The reorganization into teams and networks brought about more work through extra administrative tasks. And there were a good deal of other tasks that the middle managers had taken care of before that they were forced to leave and that the remaining employees were supposed to perform voluntarily – of course, without extra pay. From the perspective of the workers, it was clear that the demands to change their personality into a responsible co-worker only meant that they were to perform more work without more pay. Ironically, they started to talk about themselves as irresponsible counter-workers. Thereby they obstructed the management definition of a responsible co-worker.

One thing that strengthened the derision was all references to the customer, the customer's needs and the importance of satisfied customers. To be sure, the customers were the same people and departments within the authority that they had always been in contact with. For that reason, the workers could mobilize these customers in resisting management, too; for example, when it came to measures of customer satisfaction by surveys:

> Certainly, we don't have any real customers. The Administrator is a customer, they say. But they are my old mates and I have worked together with them before and the only difference now is that I have and they have masses of papers that we send back and forth. The so called customer contacts me if they want to order anything. It is not more difficult than that. And then we fill in the Customer Satisfaction Index together over a cup of coffee. They are just close by in the same house. (2005: 208, my translation)

The workers did not think either that the comprehensive view that management talked about – business is the most important thing – was reasonable. When they themselves talked about a comprehensive view, they meant that one should not put different parts of the authority against each other but instead regard it as a whole – the task of which was to serve the public.

To the workers, the demand to become responsible co-workers became a threat towards their independence and collective responsibility. Management made the worker choose between, on the one hand, the responsibility, independence, businessmanship and employability of the responsible co-worker, and, on the other, the repudiated civil servant. The workers chose the civil servant because the alternative choice simply seemed to be manipulation to get more work out of them without a pay rise.

Against the inevitable market the workers put the repudiated market, against the boundary-free organization the insatiable organization, and against the responsible co-worker the irresponsible counter-worker. Against business first, they put their dignity first.

(Huzell, 2005, 2009)

15
The Way of Doing Things

A newly hired factory worker was instructed by some workmates about her different tasks:

> OK, this is the way you are supposed to do it, but this is the way that I actually do it because it is quicker (or safer, or less tiring). But don't let the supervisor see you doing it like that, or tell him that you worked it out for yourself. Don't say that I showed you.

That was not, of course, the way to do the job that had been decided by management.

(White, 1988)

16
The Boiler Struggle

In the factory, sulphate cellulose was boiled. Enormous boilers were filled with wood chips, chemicals and steam. The mixture was boiled for about four hours into pulp, whereupon the boiler was emptied, cleaned and filled again. The greatest work efforts were required when the boil was started and when the boiler was emptied. Between those tasks, it was fairly calm – or, more correctly, it would have been fairly calm if there had been only one boiler. However, there were three. So, during the time the boil was running in boiler number 1, a new boil was started in number 2, and while that was running, another one was started in number 3. Thus, the calm periods were neither very long nor frequent. The workers thought that three was the maximum possible number of boilers that they could handle.

However, management thought differently. The workers had so much time left over, they claimed, that it would be possible to install a fourth boiler. The workers protested as that would lead to harder work and stronger management control, but this did not help. An additional boiler was put into operation. To begin with, the new installation did not increase production – the workers simply made sure that they did not do any more work. In doing so, they demonstrated every day that they were right when they claimed that three boils was the maximum possible during a shift. The next shift did the same. And the next. As the years went by, it became clear, however, that the workers could not maintain this resistance to control and drudgery. Gradually, the time for each boil was reduced and production went up, and finally, four boils were carried out during each shift.

Then management installed a fifth boiler. The boiler struggle started all over again, following the same pattern as before. At first there was no increase in output, but slowly the workers were forced to increase the intensity of their work.

The whole course of events took 20 years. Management never understood that the workers were not trying to restrict production for the sake of it, or to have an easy time. It did not realize that the workers' resistance was directed against the greater level of management control and the heavier workload. It did not comprehend that their misbehaviour was a rational expression of their efforts to keep their dignity. Therefore, management did not seek the workers' opinions and advice – they were not given any influence over any decisions that concerned their work. Management just forced the new boilers on them. If management had taken the workers' arguments into consideration, things might have been different. This could, for example, have made management shift its focus away from how to control the workers and pressure them into working harder towards how to break the connection between productivity and drudgery. Instead, neglecting its workers' dignity for 20 years has cost the company the equivalent of five and a half years of production.

(Skorstad, 2002)

17
The Company in Trouble

The company was in constant trouble. Its customers were large motor-vehicle producers with a strong position in the market. They autocratically laid down the conditions of sale and delivery times, as well as the quality and quantity of the products. At the same time, the company did not have a corresponding position with its own subcontractors and had to accept deficiencies in deliveries. In particular, there was a problem with some defects that were only cosmetic but had not been accepted by the company's customers. In addition, the company's technical equipment was quite temperamental, which caused frequent interruptions to the flow of production. One of the workers had three posters ready to put up above his machine. The first one read, 'Out of order'; the second, 'Still out of order'; and the third, 'For sale: modern Japanese machine; could be repaired or used for spare parts'.

Senior management had based the organization of work on detailed prescriptions of operating procedures and tight surveillance of workers. Above each work station there was a sheet of paper containing step-by-step instructions that were to be followed meticulously. People from the quality-control department patrolled the lines, checking that the workers were complying with the work standards. There were also several control stages concerning product quality. Finally, there was a traceability system in place, which made it possible to trace any produced item back to the worker who was responsible for it.

The workers, the supervisors and probably some of the junior managers were aware that the workflow would be impossible to maintain if production were to be carried out according to senior management directives. They had to conspire in order to 'fiddle' with the work to get it done efficiently. In order to do so, they had to evade the surveillance, both collectively and individually. A number of units were, for example, to be randomly selected in order to quality control a batch, but the workers cooperated by choosing those that would pass the control, while letting units with such small blemishes that the customers would not notice proceed along the line. The controller also sent defective units directly back to the responsible operator for rectification, without registering it on the system. The supervisors participated in ways like these to escape parts of the surveillance. Another way to improve the workflow was to find shortcuts around the prescribed standards. At the same time, workers not complying with this group discipline were regarded as 'skivers' and sloppy, and they were sanctioned by the others. By 'making time' in this way, they created some space and some autonomy, which enabled work to be smooth and efficient in spite of surveillance and senior management's work standards.

(Webb and Palmer, 1998)

18
Management Resistance to Change

We are in a wooden toy factory. In one section of the production process, partly assembled toys are being spray-painted and then hung on hooks that move them through an oven to dry them. All the workers are women and the department is known for high absence levels and labour turnover combined with low morale and low profits.

The women are sitting in front of an endless row of constantly moving hooks. The speed with which the hooks pass by is calculated precisely by engineers to make it possible for a trained worker to hang a toy on a hook before it passes by. But the women cannot fill each hook on time; many hooks go into the oven empty. In the past, they complained that the pace was too high and that the engineers had set the line at an impossible speed. Several of them quit their jobs and had to be replaced by new employees. The foreman called a meeting in order to start a discussion among the women about what could be done. The result was that the workers suggested that the pace of the line should vary depending on how they felt at different times of the shift. They were not machines, they were human beings. The engineers were not happy; they used terms like 'heresy' to condemn the notion that a number of unskilled women would have a better idea about the scientifically calculated speed. After long and difficult discussions with the supervisor, it was finally decided that the experiment was to be implemented.

The foreman had a control installed that had a three-speed dial: slow, medium and fast. The workers could now regulate the pace of the hooks. They were delighted about this control and used their lunch breaks to discuss how fast they would make the hooks go at different times of the day. Soon, the following pattern emerged: for the first 30 minutes of the shift, the line would be driven at what the workers called medium speed, which was a bit faster in reality than 'medium' on the control. They then sped up the line until just before and after lunch, when they went down to slow. For the rest of the shift, they gradually sped up the pace until the last half hour, when it was set at medium.

The result was that the workers reported a much greater level of work satisfaction while efficiency and productivity also rose drastically, as did the department's profits. The pace of the hooks set by the engineers was just below the position of 'medium' on the control panel, while the average speed at which the workers ran the line was considerably higher. Few hooks, or none at all, went into the oven empty, while the number of rejects did not increase. Within three weeks, the women had produced at a level that was between 30 and 50 per cent higher than before, something that had an effect on their wages: now they were making more than many other workers in the factory.

So far, this is a charming little story, but here it changes. Other employees started to complain about the 'imbalance' in wages – it was not regarded to be reasonable that unskilled women had higher wages than skilled men. The engineers felt that their prestige was under threat and some management prerogatives were in danger. The whole situation ended up with the supervisor, in spite of the higher profits and without consulting the workers, taking away the control panel and reintroducing the old work organization. Once again, the hooks moved at a constant, time-studied pace; production fell and, within a month, six of the eight workers had found themselves new jobs. Management had resisted an organizational change that was initiated from below and that involved substantial elements of worker autonomy. This resistance made it possible for management to regain control, even though this disregarded efficiency, productivity and profit.

(Strauss, 1955)

19
The Plant Managers' Rational Resistance

The textile plants were parts of a corporation, which issued instructions about the organization of work. Often there were demands for reorganization in order to increase efficiency and profit. The instructions were to be converted by plant managers into actual changes. However, the plant managers were chastened and they saw the corporate directives as expressions of new organizational fads. One of them reacted like this: 'The CEO discovers something new, tells everyone that we need to use it, explains what happens if we don't use, calls in some outsiders [consultants] to show us how to set it up, then expects us to do the rest.' But the directives still had to be put into effect. According to the corporate plan, the reason for the change was that overall efficiency at the corporate level had to be strengthened. Corporate managers pointed in particular to the need to reduce the time it took to manufacture a product and then distribute it to the customer, while simultaneously improving quality. This required a reorganization into teamwork, especially as issues of quality could then be built into the responsibilities of the teams, rather than controlled post-production. All this would promote flexibility and enable constant adaptation to capricious markets. The corporation would shift from competing purely on low costs to a combination of low costs and product differentiation.

At the beginning, the plant managers and their production managers followed the directives of the corporate level. The corporate managers were satisfied with the result: the figures showed a positive outcome from the reorganization. However, the plant managers were not pleased at all. There were running-in costs and initial problems, which burdened the plant's results and thus affected their bonuses negatively. One of them explained:

> Personally I liked the idea of teams since it made sense to try something like that. But what worried me was the lag before positive results showed. We were told about this in the late spring. I figured a couple of months of start-up problems, then 2–3 months to iron out the difficulties. That's not too bad. The problem is that I'm losing about three months of efficiency that the company will probably forget about at the end of the year. I talked with the CFO about this and he said don't worry. But I did worry and sure enough at the end of the year my bonus was way down because our production was so low. (14)

The plant managers' implementation of the corporate managers' intentions led to better goal fulfilment at the corporate level but increased costs at the plant level. The bonus system was based on measuring and evaluating certain parts of the plant managers' performance, but the overarching goals were not included. From their point of view, it was thus rational to resist what the corporate managers wanted and to make organizational changes instead in ways that would be registered in the bonus system. That was also what happened.

Assisted by the production managers, the plant managers started to make 'adjustments' to the way work was being organized, especially regarding the teams. The autonomy of the teams was restricted and more emphasis was put on things that were part of bonus measurement: not the overall flexibility, but higher productivity, cost-cutting through fewer supervisors and higher quality. In doing so, they would be able to deliver what provided the plant managers with favourable ratios, and made their bonuses increase.

The corporate bonus system was unable to measure the contribution made by each plant to the corporate result. Therefore, the work of the plant managers was not visible in a fair way in its system of valuing work efforts – and the prime symbol for managerial dignity at work, the size of the bonus, was reduced drastically. What was rational for the corporation was no longer rational for the plant managers. Resistance was, from their point of view, the rational action to take.

(Taplin, 2001)

20
The Janitors in Silicon Valley

The so-called new economy's prestigious workplaces in the capital of the electronics industry, Silicon Valley, have to be cleaned too. They are cleaned at night, mainly by illegal immigrants. At Sonix, one of the biggest and most flourishing high-tech companies, management contracted several small non-unionized cleaning firms to do the cleaning. One of these firms was Bay-Clean. Most of its employees came from Mexico, worked for very low wages and had no benefits – not even health insurance.

Often, the equipment they were given to do the cleaning was inadequate. They were told to 'borrow' napkins from a close-by cafeteria instead of wearing out the scouring cloths. The employees who complained were assigned the worst jobs. At the same time, management required high-quality cleaning. An employee commented: 'They [supervisors] keep demanding us to work harder and faster but they do not give us the materials to do it. They want us to clean with only water and expect that everything shine!' The employees thought that the scarcity of cleaning equipment, the deficiencies of the antiquated tools they had, the supervisors' insufficient understanding of what they needed in order to do their work, and the lack of clear and fair principles for distributing the workload and setting wage rates all had one single cause: the Bay-Clean managers were unprofessional. Even worse was the fact that management did not have any respect for the workers. The cleaners complained that they had to endure insults and threats, which were direct attacks on their personal dignity.

Finally, some of them decided to get in touch with the union that had recently carried out a successful campaign against Apple

Computers in Silicon Valley, called 'Justice for Janitors'. With the help of the union, about 30 Bay-Clean cleaners took part in a rally outside the firm's office. Grudgingly, the president agreed to meet a couple of representatives of the employees, who handed over a list of demands for improving working conditions. The only result of this meeting, however, was that the cleaners whom management had identified as union sympathizers were transferred to the very worst jobs. Then management carried out an anti-union campaign and threatened to report those who joined to the immigration authorities, which would result in them losing their jobs and being sent back to Mexico.

The union responded by organizing a much bigger demonstration, this time outside the head office of Sonix. The media were invited and the cleaners' cause was presented as a question of fairness for the poorest people working in Silicon Valley. The senior management of Sonix began to fear negative publicity and soon announced that they would restructure the cleaning service by hiring a single union firm to take care of all cleaning. One result of this was that Bay-Clean went bankrupt, while most of its former employees found new jobs at the new firm, CLS. However, the cleaners' dignity was not restored as they had hoped. CLS cut down the number of employees while increasing the workload of those who remained without increasing the time allowed to do the job. One of them said, using ironic intonation:

> For example, this week we were shown some videos to teach us how to do our job properly that lasted about 30 to 45 minutes. I was laughing because the person in the video who is cleaning does everything very methodically, very slow, but in our work we have to hurry up every night to clean all the area we are assigned. (45)

The paradox of cleaning more and better in a shorter time led to a new wave of resistance and organizational misbehaviour. The management of CLS was not regarded as any more professional than that of Bay-Clean.

Then one day, the immigration authorities arrived at CLS to check the employees' papers. The union could not do anything to prevent almost all the employees from losing their jobs. Soon they were replaced by new undocumented immigrants – the difference being, however, that the new workers were paid less. Many of the previous cleaners thought that CLS itself had called in the authorities in order to achieve a wage cut. Others thought that the firm had only reaped the benefits of the situation. But no one knew for certain – just that they had lost their jobs.

(Zlolniski, 2003)

21
Managing Out, Managing Up and Managing Down

An American bank had speculated in order to generate high profits and had taken risks that were far too big. Senior management had also refrained from investing in new technology. The result was a financial crisis. The ones who got the blame, however, were the employees, especially middle managers: they did not work hard enough and they had a flawed culture, said senior management. A far-reaching reorganization was launched, by means of which all middle managers would be retrained to become change agents who would introduce the new system and the new culture in order to raise the intensity of the work. In the bank's own terminology, there were three activities in particular that they were to devote themselves to: 'managing out, managing up and managing down'. Officially, the bank's policy was that nobody would be dismissed in spite of the obvious need to reduce the number of staff. Instead, staff cuts would be achieved through attrition, which was what 'managing down' meant. In reality, there was an advanced system for getting rid of staff through the extensive measurement of their performance and then classifying them according to a statistically 'normal distribution': 15 per cent ended up at the bottom, 15 per cent at the top and 70 per cent in between. Those at the bottom were described as immature, the others as mature. After each measurement was taken, the immature were to be sacked – 'managed out'. All the others were to be 'managed up', which did not mean that they would be promoted but that their productivity would be raised.

Senior management organized comprehensive training courses for middle managers. They would be schooled in the new banking culture – a culture that would result in a more aggressive, more competitive and more profitable bank. The training sessions led to a consensus between senior and junior managers that higher productivity was necessary. There was also, however, a consensus among middle managers that led them into conflict with senior management: they agreed that methods other than those senior management was spreading via the new culture would be necessary in order to achieve this goal. An important part of the methods being taught was 'minimum job requirements'. These requirements would be decided by the managers and could vary from employee to employee – including between those with the same jobs. There would, then, no longer be job descriptions. One of the most important tasks of the managers was to use their own creativity to constantly stretch out the minimum job requirements in order to raise productivity. The middle managers were of the opinion, however, that this would lead not to higher productivity but to chaos. There had to be a standardized system of job requirements if they were to be able to evaluate employee performance. They feared that the new system would lead to pure arbitrariness and thus to strong negative reactions from their subordinates. This resistance would also be stronger when the employees discovered that all the talk about attrition was only a smokescreen behind which people were, in fact, being sacked. The prerequisite for the new programme to be successful was, they felt, that each manager would be regarded as legitimate by his or her subordinates. But the programme itself undermined this legitimacy. Top management's message was met with open organizational misbehaviour through fierce debates during training sessions.

In spite of this resistance, top management implemented its plans. The middle managers' resistance to these expressions of the new culture during training thus developed into resistance to its practice. The instructions of the new banking culture included the middle managers having to manage out non-productive and immature employees from the organization. They also had to make sure that the mature employees would be stretched out by continuously extending the minimum job requirements. They chose, however, a different way of achieving the goal of higher productivity. They tried to avoid both managing out and stretching out. Instead, they strove to establish consent and stability in order to increase performance: they went for managing up.

Many bank branches were closed down, but all the branch managers who remained fought in order to not encounter the same misfortune by reaching high productivity numbers. They did this in many ways, all of which were intended to improve the results of the whole branch rather than those of individuals. One way of doing this was to encourage employees to attend training courses so that everyone could perform more tasks. Another was to delegate responsibility while at the same time doing shifts themselves as tellers. The branch managers also organized short meetings at the beginning of each working day to plan the most efficient performance of the tasks. Instead of hiding top management's continuous downsizing, they accurately showed the information that they had – something that was another reason for the employees to increase their efforts. In their resistance to top management, the branch managers mobilized the support of the employees, even though the employees sometimes protested and resisted against some measures. The branch managers were convinced, however, that top management's ways would have led to even stronger resistance and may have jeopardized the survival of the whole bank.

(Smith, 1990)

22
The Faulty Switches

The tests at the end of the line for assembling switches for industrial machines were showing more and more often that these were faulty. They were returned to the workers for re-assembly. Soon, the workers requested that the line be stopped while they tried to find out what was wrong. They then discovered that a tiny component was often faulty, so the charge hand sent for a production engineer. While waiting for him, the workers assembled ten switches using faulty components and ten using fault-free components. When the switches were tested, the first ten turned out to be non-functional while the last ten went through quality control without problems. However, the production engineer did not believe in these results or the workers' explanation of the fault. He spent a lot of time going through all the components, looking disdainful the whole time – while the line stood still.

When the workers returned the next morning, the charge hand told them that, in fact, it was the component they had singled out as the culprit that was responsible for the problem and that it was going to be scrapped. A researcher who happened to be present asked them why they had not simply kept assembling the switches, letting the engineer take the blame when they were returned by the customers. Why had they bothered? The answer was that it would have harmed the company's reputation – and besides, who wants to do a bad job? They had also had a break from the line while militating against part of management's power by demonstrating the incompetence of a superior; especially as it concerned the quality of the products that management had always cherished so much.

(White, 1988)

23
Being Best

Since acquiring American owners, ElectroSystems had been shedding jobs for more than ten years, while increasing the intensity of work substantially. Yet it was constantly losing market share. In the eyes of the employees, the changes not only entailed sackings and poorer working conditions for those remaining, but also meant that they were forced to let products of inferior quality slip through. An employee expressed her feelings thus: 'You can't take pride in your work, you can't have work satisfaction when you see some of the jobs that get past. "Oh, that's good enough," they say.' There was no doubt: the company's problems were due to management incompetence. 'It's management's job to run the factory, not ours. What else do they get higher pay for?' Management was not doing its job in the eyes of the workers.

Management was of the opinion that the problems were due to the employees not working hard enough. In order to stimulate them into exerting themselves more, they launched a campaign on the theme of 'ElectroSystems – Aiming to be the best'. Comments made by the employees include these:

> 'What do they mean – *aiming* to be best? These Americans don't seem to know that we used to *be* the best. We aren't any more.'

> 'This kind of nonsense may be effective with American workers, but we know who's responsible for us not being the best any longer – management!'

(White, 1988)

24
The Tool Crib

The workers at this American machine shop were convinced that it was impossible to 'make out' on the piece work jobs if they followed management's instructions. Instead, they had to find 'angels' in order to 'fix' the piece rate. In practice that meant that the operators did their job in collaboration with several other occupational groups, mainly the set-up men, the inspectors, the tool-crib attendants, the stockmen and the time-checkers. Most of this collaboration was hidden from management and, as a result, the workers had built up some autonomy from the control that management thought it was exercising.

This collaboration involved the operators keeping the tools they needed in work instead of returning them to the tool crib as they were supposed to according to management rules. This made the job easier and more efficient, as well as enabling them to fix their piece work. But one day, management introduced a new system for the tool crib – one that would make it possible for management to control this part of the labour process. Every worker who fetched equipment from the tool crib had to sign a receipt and two copies. The original was to be kept in the tool crib, with one copy going to the worker. When the equipment was returned, the worker was to be handed the original as proof that he had not retained any of the tools. At the same time, no new equipment was to be handed out until the used tool had been returned. In that way, there would be order, and opportunities of fiddling with the piece rate would diminish.

Part of fixing the piece rate consisted of fetching the tools for a new job before the old one had been registered as finished, a procedure that required the tool-crib attendants to hand out tools in advance or even allow the workers to enter the tool store to fetch them. In that way, the operators won time, work flowed better and they could make out on the piece work. All this was now much more difficult, but it soon turned out that the new system could not be maintained. The tool-crib attendants had a lot of extra work to do and, in the end, could not keep a check on all the equipment, which worker was to have what and where all the receipts were. With that, long and unproductive waiting times arose. In order to avoid this situation, the tool-crib attendants started allowing the workers into the tool crib so that they could fetch the equipment they needed. The new system broke down and the operators regained their autonomy.

Management's answer was to abolish the receipts and introduce another system, which was based on a new kind of work order. This now included the types of tool to be used, with a copy going to the tool-crib attendants. When the operators came to fetch their equipment, they had to sign the copy. Opportunities to fetch tools before new jobs were begun were inhibited since delivery of the equipment was connected to the work order. However, by means of collaborating, the workers soon got round this system too. The set-up men could move freely in the tool crib, which made it possible for them to fetch the equipment the operators needed in advance. Thus, everything went back to the normal fixing of the piece rate.

Management introduced another rule – one that prohibited everyone, except for the supervisors and tool-crib attendants, from entering the tool crib. The queues increased once again and the tool-crib attendants' workload increased substantially, with conflicts between different occupational groups intensifying. The situation became intolerable and the tool-room employees started to keep the door ajar. Set-up workers and operators were once again able to fetch what they needed to do their jobs.

The management order that the door was to be closed was still hanging on the wall of the tool crib, but nobody cared anymore. Work flowed with fixed piece rates.

If this lesson, about rational worker resistance, had been introduced into latter-day management teachings, then American and British managers would not have had to repeat the same mistake concerning tool cribs 20 or 30 years later.

(Roy, 1955; see also Burawoy, 1979 and White, 1988)

25
The Cocktail Waitresses

In this Reno casino, the surveillance system is very rigorous. Big one-way mirrors are part of the décor, more or less hidden cameras are everywhere, and cash registers and receipts are checked. Moreover, the pit bosses and casino hosts walk around to monitor what is going on at the tables and gaming machines. In this setting, a certain professional group, the cocktail waitresses, have been hired to serve free drinks to the customers. They are paid by the casino, but most of their income is from gamblers' tips (non-gamblers have to go to the bar and buy a drink if they want one).

There are also stringent rules governing the cocktail waitresses' appearance. There is a beauty requirement when it comes to make-up and figure, but also a special – and rather revealing – uniform: a very low-cut, short dress, or a low-cut vest and leotard plus a tuxedo jacket with long tails, and at least 1.5 inch heels. The cocktail waitresses' job is difficult and often stressful. They have to balance heavy trays of drinks on one arm (wearing high-heeled shoes) and carry them through crowds and confined spaces. Their working conditions can lead to less glamorous physical injuries, like carpal tunnel syndrome, back pain, bunions and hammertoes. The job also requires a lot of social manoeuvring. The cocktail waitresses must keep the bartenders happy; for example, they are expected to give them 15–20 per cent of their tips. If they are not happy, they can delay the drinks, making the gamblers surly and leading to considerably reduced tipping. And, of course, they have to persuade gamblers to be generous with their tips. The cocktail waitresses do not complain about their uniform as it is regarded as sexy and thus contributing towards higher tips. A visible tattoo or too much or too little make-up can, however, be seen as a trait indicating independence and resistance.

From management's point of view, the serving of drinks is to be done in a way that does not intrude on the customers' gambling. There are several reasons why the casino serves free liquor. One, of course, is that this attracts punters, but also management does not want gambling to be interrupted by the customer having to go to the bar for a drink – it wants to keep guests at the blackjack tables or on the one-armed bandits. Also, intoxicated customers tend to take bigger risks and play with higher stakes. From the perspective of the cocktail waitresses, the idea is to get as many tips as possible from the customers. There is the possibility of achieving this by deviating from what management wants by building up a specific relationship with particular gamblers: they do not want to leave their roulette tables or poker machines either in order to get a drink, and it is through the cocktail waitresses that they can get free drinks. This establishes a mutual dependence, within which the cocktail waitresses can manoeuvre at a distance from management surveillance.

Gamblers often fall into a trance in front of a slot machine or a gambling table, thus management wants the cocktail waitresses simply to put the drink down without disturbing the punter. This, however, would mean very bad economics for the waitress. Her trick lies not in putting the drink down but instead passing it to the gambler in such a way that they notice it and, in doing so, also become aware of the 'duty' to tip the waitress. And if that does not help, she can count her earlier tips, jingling the coins, and rattle glasses until she attracts enough attention to make the gambler notice her. If all that is in vain, her next strategy is to 'forget' the next order until it dawns on the customer exactly what is expected of them.

There are occasions when a waitress wants to get rid of a customer, and there are tricks for that too. There is one story about a noisy, non-tipping group who were constantly yelling for drinks. Trying to forget about them did not work. A brief conference with the bartender led to the decision to 'really give them what they asked for'. All their drinks were spiked with an extra shot of vodka and, within an hour, the inebriated party had staggered off to their rooms, with the waitress hoping that they would wake up the next morning with terrible hangovers.

(Bayard de Volo, 2003)

26
Forcing Off Stiffs and Keeping Georges

In Las Vegas, the glamorous mega-casinos along 'The Strip' no longer dominate the industry. Many smaller casinos have been relocated 'off-strip', turning to local people and to ordinary tourists who play for smaller stakes. Only a few of the visitors are big gamblers who take a risk – or a chance of winning, if you prefer – with large sums of money. One of those casinos is Jackpot, and this story was enacted at its blackjack tables. In order to understand it, we must know a bit about this game.

Those directly involved are the dealer, an employee of the casino whose job it is to lead the game and the gamblers, who are Jackpot's customers. The dealer plays against each player while each player plays solely against the dealer. Each round starts with the players placing their bets in the form of chips, the colours of which symbolize their monetary worth. The dealer then gives each player and him- or herself two cards. The spot cards count from two to nine, while the 10, jack, queen and king count as ten, and an ace can be either 1 or 11, according to the player's choice. The object of the game is to achieve a higher total than the dealer, but without exceeding 21. If you do, then you go bust and you lose. After the first deal, the players have to evaluate their chances and decide whether to 'hit' by taking a new card or 'stand', while at the same time deciding whether or not to bet more money. If the player has two cards of the same value, there is also the possibility of splitting the pair, to make each of them the first card in a new hand. All dealers, but not all players, know the mathematical probabilities of the different alternatives, involving, for example, that one should always split 8s but not 10s (including jacks, queens and kings). After all the players have played their hands, the dealer exposes his or her cards and plays out the hand.

At Jackpot, as at other casinos, surveillance is very thorough. A number of blackjack tables are monitored by one or two supervisors – pit bosses. There is also a black globe installed over each table containing a camera, which is connected to a control room. In spite of this, dealers often succeed in manipulating the game in such a way that they can get as many tips as possible. The players are expected to tip the dealers; however, far from all of them do. Jackpot only pays the minimum wage and the dealers' income is made up, to 75 per cent or more, from tips from customers. Tips are, then, a very important part of their job and different tricks that make customers tip heavily circulate among the dealers.

The owners of the casino have formulated three business goals: speed – every dealer is to carry out as many deals as possible in order to make Jackpot generate maximum profit; security – the casino must not be done out of money by players or employees, requiring that dealers must wear a specific uniform with a long-sleeved shirt that has tight cuffs and an apron to prevent them from pocketing chips; and service – the customers are to have a pleasant and personal experience so that they gamble more. By breaking one or two of these rules simultaneously, the dealers can get the largest tips from gamblers.

The players tip by betting on behalf of the dealer before the game begins. If the player loses, the bet goes to Jackpot; but if the player wins, the dealer gets both the bet and the winnings. The many and very detailed regulations governing the dealers' conduct include their not being allowed to give advice to the punters regarding the best way of playing. It is prohibited to even hint that one should split 8s but not 10s. Furthermore, the dealer has to make sure that the player feels welcome by attending to them as individuals. Here is an example of the owners' service goals being compatible with the dealers' desire to get tips:

> Kim, a young Vietnamese dealer of 2 years, understands immediately that the two businessmen who have just sat down at her table expect friendly smiles and entertaining small talk. She provides both and they fulfil their end of the bargain: the two men tip frequently and well. Soon, though, they both lose several large hands

and become irritable. Now her smiles are inappropriate. 'Why are you so happy? Do you like to see us lose like this?' She becomes quiet and serious, dealing quickly and without expression as the two men play their hands intensely. Soon they have won their original money back and more. The cocktails take effect and they now are loud and boisterous. Kim laughs along with them, occasionally cracking jokes herself. The cycle repeats several times, as it does every night. (419)

At the same time, it is strictly prohibited to try to make players tip, or to treat those who do not differently from those who do. But for the dealers, having such influence is extremely important, despite it being controlled so strongly.

The dealers and the pit bosses, who once were dealers and who sometimes still step into that role during unexpected peaks, divide the players into different categories. In one of these, they differentiate between those who tip (georges) and those who do not (stiffs); in another they distinguish between high-rollers and low-rollers, depending on how much money they bet. Both the dealers and the pit bosses behave differently towards the different categories. Almost all players are low-rollers – a dealer can do several shifts without a high-roller turning up. When it comes to low-rollers, the pit bosses leave the games to the dealers, providing them with the opportunity to use two tip-generating tricks. One is to let the georges win as much as possible to make them continue to be generous, the other to force the stiffs away from the table to be replaced by georges. A dealer can help a player to win by giving advice, although this must be done cautiously because it is prohibited. For example, if a player is about to split two 10s, the dealer can ask: 'Are you sure you want to do that?' Or when the player asks for another card in a situation that means a big risk of losing, the dealer can advise: 'Now be careful here.'

Another ploy is to keep count of how many cards have been dealt that are worth ten. The more 10s that are left in the deck, the more advantageous it is for the player – the fewer, the more profitable it is for the casino. According to the rules, the deck is to be shuffled two-thirds of the way through, but the dealer can bring a player extra winnings by shuffling earlier or later – depending on the odds in relation to the number of 10s. The tactic used against stiffs is the opposite. The dealers let them split 10s and keep 8s without comment. They can also deal extra quickly as they know that the odds are on the casino's side in the long run: the more hands are played, the more likely it is that the stiff will lose. And the dealer can shuffle the deck when it is least advantageous to the player.

As we have seen, the extreme low-wage policy of the owners of Jackpot makes tips crucial for the dealers. Therefore, they ignore the security objectives when these relate to georges: the dealers let them win to keep them at the table. In relation to stiffs, they ignore the service objective instead: the dealers make them lose as much as possible and as fast as possible to get rid of them. The owners' objectives become contradictory when implemented at the blackjack tables.

But the dealers' tactics only work in relation to low-rollers. When it comes to high-rollers, things are quite different. As soon as a player makes a big bet, the dynamic at the table becomes much altered. If the bet is, for example, a brown chip, which is equivalent to $100, the dealer has to call out 'Brown plays!', upon which the pit boss quickly shows up and the cameras zoom in. Supervision intensifies and there is no possibility for the dealer to manipulate the game – independently of the player being a stiff or a george. Not even the usually inventive dealers can do anything about the high-rollers.

(Sallaz, 2002)

27
The Evil Spirits

In this Malaysian free-zone, there were three Japanese electronics companies. Most of their work consisted of assembling small components – small enough for the workers to have to use microscopes to perform their tasks. All were women because, as it said in an advertising brochure for the free-zone, 'Her hands are small and she works fast with extreme care. Who, therefore, could be better qualified by nature and inheritance to contribute to the efficiency of a bench assembly production line than the oriental girl?' The fact that the young women were first-generation industrial workers and had been brought up by their rural families to be compliant and deferent was also an advantage. Furthermore, they could be paid much lower wages than male workers. It was also good that they had poor education because, as a chief engineer put it: 'The highly educated person is very difficult to control.' Finally, the women ought not be married because that could distract them from their work.

The working hours were very long, demands to work overtime were common, the work was monotonous and boring, and the discipline was harsh. Many of the supervisors swore and shouted in order to increase productivity, and the women were afraid of them. Often, the only possible reaction after such a scolding was to weep quietly. They had never encountered such treatment prior to becoming industrial workers and they felt that this discipline was a threat to their entire human dignity. But it also led them to consciously reduce the pace of their work or to be careless when assembling the components, not to mention feigning total stupidity when the foremen gave them new orders. One way out of this, to be able to rest for a while, was to

81

mention 'women's problems', which could only be taken care of in the locker room. Also, women went as far as wreaking vengeance on the supervisors by destroying components or sabotaging machines.

Increasingly often, the women were being possessed by evil spirits. They cried and fought against these spirits, flailing backwards and forwards, falling to the ground in spasms. Finally, they had to be sent home. Management blamed the whole thing on mass hysteria. However, it hired an exorcist who was to free the factory of spirits by splashing holy water around and killing chickens. But the spirits returned. Eventually, management decided that workers who became possessed by spirits for a third time were to be fired. Not even evil spirits were much help against the capitalist factory discipline and the insults of the foremen.

(Ong, 1987)

28
The Rules of the Restaurant

This restaurant chain has extensive and rigorous rules about many things, but at the restaurant in New Jersey, nobody cares very much.

For the waitresses, the rules concern, for example, how many croutons to put on a salad, what to say when greeting the customers, how long their earrings may be, where on the uniform their nametags are to be attached, when and how often they have to check on the customers once the entrée has been served, when and how to clear dirty plates off the table, how much ice to put in a soft drink, and the colour of their shoes and whether or not they can have stripes on them. Each waitress has to attend training courses to learn the rules and practice working according to them. However, at the New Jersey restaurant, the rules are not followed and nobody attends the courses. The waitresses try to maintain their autonomy and they succeed in avoiding most of the rules and regulations.

Their strong position owes much to the fact that in New Jersey restaurants are relentlessly competing with each other over manpower, which is why it is a waitresses' labour market. There is a constant shortage and the sign in the window of the restaurant saying that help is wanted is never removed. Any waitress who is dissatisfied with her working conditions can leave a job knowing full well that she can get another one tomorrow, resulting in a very high staff churn. There is no time at the New Jersey restaurant to teach loads of rules or how to apply them. Immediately after being hired, waitresses have to start working. They are 'thrown on the floor', to use their own expression, which results in their doing things their own way.

Management churn is also high as there is seldom time to devote oneself to managerial or administrative work. Instead, managers repeatedly have to fill gaps when staff are missing from dish-washing duties, waitressing duties or the kitchen. They do not have the skills of waitresses or cooks, but seeing a man in a suit and tie clearing tables of dirty dishes, sorting silverware, emptying the garbage or running errands for waitresses is common. It is not possible for managers to build a strong position of authority with regard to their waitresses under such circumstances.

As a consequence of management problems, there are very seldom enough supplies to serve all the guests. There is not only a lack of staff but also of raw materials, serving dishes, soup bowls, tablecloths and so on. This contributes to management's trouble with upholding the rules. Reactions to such demands can be as follows:

> You're going to sit here and yap at me because my earrings hang an inch too long ... or maybe I have one hair out of place, or I have fingernail polish on? Over everything in the store, where I have no silverware, no glasses, and so forth, you're going to give me a half an hour lecture on fingernail polish? (81)

All the waitresses agree that all the problems they encounter while working are due to management's incompetence. The reason that the job gets done at all, and that the guests are satisfied, is that the waitresses work in their own way, ignoring the restaurant's rules. That is, at least, what the waitresses think.

(Paules, 1991)

29
A Song against Monotony

Working in this blind factory is really boring. Among the workers, what can be called a 'staying-alive' culture has emerged – one that has as its aim trying to joke, laugh, sing and have fun in order to make it through the working day. One expression of this culture is the fact that music is played on radios and CD players right through all the shifts. The most popular song is 'We've Got to Get Out of this Place' by The Animals. At the start of the lyric, the singer describes how he, as a young man, saw his father being ground down by his work and that this is what is threatening to happen to him, too. The chorus shows how to be saved from monotonous work:

> We've got to get out of this place
> If it's the last thing we ever do
> We've got to get out of this place,
> There's a better life for me and you

'You are worth more than this job,' the song says. 'You have to get out of here to regain your dignity.' Other songs that met with approval, and strengthened the staying-alive culture, had titles like 'I Will Survive' and 'Dignity'.

One of the new workers decided to leave after only six weeks. 'I've had enough, I can't take it here,' he said. He also wrote a song about his experiences of working at the blind factory:

> Working for the shark,
> Dodging his back when the sky goes dark,

Bobbing and weaving for the time it will take
'Cos our minds are rocks and they will not break.
Same old jazz day in and day out,
Will make us run and scream and shout.
The sixth week of boredom slowly it's passed
When the clock strikes one they can kiss my ass.

(Korczynski, 2007)

30
Hebrew Slaves

The meatpackers are very busy. They work silently and intensively. Suddenly, one of them starts humming the 'Chorus of the Hebrew Slaves' from the Verdi opera *Nabucco*. Soon the others join in. The singing is interrupted by one of the workers asking for materials that should be there but are not. The hard work continues in silence until another worker starts humming 'Please, Release Me'. They all join in. Then there is a Swedish song: 'Let the Prisoners Out, Spring is Here!'

(Strömberg and Karlsson, 2009)

31
The Adroit Middle Manager

In the office of a government agency, a serious health hazard appeared, but the executive management did not think they could afford to do anything about it. One of the middle managers, Maria, was told by a group of professionals that the employees were planning a wild strike in answer to the inaction of management with regard to the safety problems. Others had been in contact with the media. In this situation, senior management demanded that middle managers inform the employees that it was a false alarm – that there was no problem, no health hazard. Maria objected by saying that it could very well be a real risk and that it was not very wise to lie to the employees. Senior management dismissed her arguments and the other middle managers did as they were ordered: 'There is no danger,' they told their subordinates.

The group of professionals warned Maria that the strike was imminent. She tried once more to convince senior management that a strategy other than denying the hazard was required, but in vain. She then realized that in order to be able to handle the employees' resistance against the health risk, she had to resist the executive management by being honest. She knew highly placed people in a management and budget agency to whom she spoke secretly. They became worried about a possible loss of productivity and, as early as the next day, they conducted an unannounced inspection of Maria's agency. Soon, other inspectors also showed up to investigate the situation. Additionally, senior management was confronted by journalists and politicians. It soon turned out to be possible, after all, to take care of the problem within the limits of the budget.

Maria's adroit manoeuvring within her social networks had solved the situation, and the threat to the health of the employees was removed this time.

(Brower and Abolfia, 1995)

32
The Workplace That Was to Be Like a Kindergarten

The word 'paternalism' stands for an overprotective mentality, paternal protection in exchange for loyalty and obedience. In working life, it implies a relationship between management and workers that reminds us of that between parents and children, teachers and pupils, or masters and servants. Still, this is part of rather modern international management philosophies.

At this company, which we can call Sunray, management was very aware that the work carried out in the offices was extremely dreary and monotonous. However, instead of trying to change the work environment, it concentrated on creating a culture based on paternalism. This culture would help to achieve high productivity and efficiency, in spite of the undignified work – such was the idea, especially on the part of the owner and the HR department. There was to be a nice, fun-filled and festive atmosphere, with positive attitudes among the employees. Many steps were taken to create and support this. One of these involved the furnishings, which, through happy and bright colours, would generate a blissful milieu. The walls were yellow and red, the supporting pillars were purple and the floors were bright blue.

Informal dress would contribute to the party-like atmosphere. Other indications were that the employees were encouraged to dye their hair bright orange and to have visible tattoos and facial piercings. 'Here, there is none of the boring appearance of other offices! Here, we have fun!' Special team-building exercises would bring an extra sense of community spirit, combined with theme days when the employees would dress up as their favourite heroes of the screen or comic-strip characters. Sometimes an Away Day was arranged, when they all went somewhere to set up a play – or as one of the managers put it, a 'kind of school musical' – taking its point of departure in the mission statement of the company. The employees would experience an outflow of childish creativity in the service of the company. It was also important that the employees regarded the company as a happy family. For example, all educational materials talked about the 'Sunray family'.

All the employees who, on this basis, regarded the company to be a fun-filled, happy and shared family were regarded to have the right attitude. The wrong attitude could, together with deficiencies in productivity, lead to dismissal. The corporate culture was about indoctrinating the employees into becoming the company's children, in a state of dependence. An HR manager was convinced that this had been successful. She said: 'I can't believe anyone would say that what we do is garbage. It's impossible – since I would not have selected people who thought like that in the first place.' The very selection of employees ought to guarantee the triumph of this paternalistic culture – and all measures taken on behalf of management ought to guarantee success.

But things did not turn out that way. There were employees who had been incorporated into the Sunray culture and who had the right attitude, but there were also those who resisted it. Their resistance was not very dramatic; it was rather unobtrusive. The main expression of misbehaviour was cynical withdrawal, entailing that these employees refused to be defined as children or to accept the identity of being dependent. They did not have much respect for management and refused to regard their superiors as father figures or teachers. They thought that their dignity was being threatened by such a culture. Instead, they stressed the fact that they were grown-up, responsible and worthy human beings – at work too. Management spoke a lot about empowering the employees, but this rhetoric did not correspond very well with the corporate culture, which it was simultaneously fostering in order to make the workplace like a kindergarten. For example, one woman preferred to go sick to participate in a theme day that included fancy dress. She considered it humiliating to be forced to take part in such games. It was difficult enough to maintain her dignity in her day-to-day work – even less so when kitted out as Wonder Woman.

(Fleming, 2005a, 2005b)

33
The Roaming Russian Dolls

The web design department of an international IT firm was going to be a fun workplace – that is what management had decided. The customers were going to be really impressed by the unconventional and creative style of the department. This would be noticeable in the architectural layout; for example, the elliptical corridor that divided up the premises diagonally and that was lit by blue lighting. There was also a particularly fun room, furnished like a children's playroom. The whole office was strewn with toys, games, sculptures and even a fully equipped billiard table. The most fun, impressive and creative thing, however, was that management had obtained a set of very expensive human-sized Russian dolls to ornament the workplace.

Management also succeeded in spreading its message in connection with a TV programme about the department. Together with the producer, management was able to persuade some employees to participate in a feigned brainstorming session concerning a customer's website, which included playing with Lego bricks during intense discussions.

The employees appreciated some parts of the fun, but mostly they felt humiliated. They regarded themselves as serious professionals, who were proud of their work and what they produced. It seemed like an insult to them that playrooms, silly corridors and big Russian dolls were necessary to make their creativity flow – it was unworthy of their professionalism.

One thing that strengthened the impression of superficiality was the fact that nothing had changed in the organization of the work itself. Management still exerted strong and meticulous control and refused to relinquish any of its decision-making power. It was management who had decided that it was going to be a fun workplace. This was a kind of prescribed or designed fun and the employees did not have any real influence over which fun things to purchase. Moreover, the Russian dolls happened to arrive unannounced at a time when management was reducing the budget for items that the employees regarded to be necessities. This was a matter of, for example, the staff asking for a kitchenette to make tea and prepare food when they had to work overtime in evenings and at weekends in order to meet deadlines. But management thought this would be too expensive. The department could not even afford a kettle for its employees.

Then, the Russian dolls started to roam the premises. They turned up in the least expected places. For example, a female employee called security late one evening as she was certain there was a man in the ladies' room. When the security guard had a look, it turned out to be one of the male Russian dolls that had been put in a cubicle. On another occasion, a customer was somewhat surprised when the lift doors opened and he found himself standing in front of five giant dolls. Management did not think this was fun at all. They banned the employees from playing with the dolls. However, playing with the dolls became even wilder. The dolls started showing marks caused by punches to their faces. Management let it be known that this was regarded as damage to company property, and if those responsible were found out, they would be dismissed immediately.

Management did not understand the employees' reactions as they tried to preserve their dignity. Instead of taking them seriously, it increased the level of control by installing CCTV cameras. But that did not create more fun, even if it did prevent the Russian dolls from roaming.

(Warren and Fineman, 1997)

34
The Surveillance Cameras and Regular Customers

The owner of the exotic dance club was, of course, out to make as much money as possible from the female dancers' bodies. Part of that involved installing surveillance cameras everywhere to make it possible for him and the bosses to detect the slightest violation of the rules he had laid down. For each crime, a fine was imposed, payable to the owner. The most serious crime was to break the rule that stated that the owner gets a certain proportion of the tips that the strippers get from their customers.

The cameras were positioned in such a way that they could zoom in on every nook and cranny of the premises (or almost every nook and cranny, as we will see). The dancers were aware the whole time that their smallest movements could be closely studied on the screens in the office. It filled them with horror to be called up there to get a telling-off, or to be fined or even fired. In this way, the owner seemed to have removed every possible way for the dancers to act independently. Resistance seemed impossible, but it still existed.

Organizational misbehaviour occurred in collusion with the regulars. The regulars were quite familiar with the club's financial system and the existence of the cameras, but they wanted to give 'their' dancer extra money without the cameras being able to register the transaction. One way to do this was in the special 'lap dancing' room. Here, the dancer sits on the lap of the customer and grinds his crotch. At this club, the cost was $20 if she was topless, with $5 going to the owner. If she was totally nude, the price was $40, and this time $10 went to the owner. The trick was for the customer to put a note under one of his legs and, during the dance, the dancer would then bend forward, protecting this move by turning her back to the camera, and take the money.

The dancers had also located particular corners that were not covered by the cameras, especially in the almost dark so-called Champagne room, to which they could lead their regulars. Of course, this still involved a risk, but one of them explained:

> Look Vincent [the owner] isn't the one out here dealing with people ... he fucking makes a shit load here. So if I can make extra money there is no fucking way I am going to not do it. I have a kid and I am going to school and I need the money. I already pay him to make my schedule and pay him for my dances where I use my body and I refuse to not make extra when I can. The rules here are ridiculous! I am careful ... you know, but I still do it. (312)

Sometimes, then, the dancers succeeded in escaping surveillance with the help of the regulars. However, in other situations, they could make use of the cameras themselves, such as when a customer became too demanding and wanted special sexual services. The dancer did not want to lose him as a source of income and thus could not turn him down brusquely. Instead, she said that she really wanted the same thing but that it was against the rules and the cameras saw everything that happened ... Unfortunately, it was impossible for her to do as he wanted.

Thus, now and then, the dancers could – in collaboration with the regulars – escape the surveillance cameras, but they could also use them as protection against pushy customers.

(Egan, 2004)

35
Sticks and Rotten Carrots

The latest from the management of the restaurant at this international hotel was the introduction of Service Standards, detailing the way in which the workers were to work and pointing out the skills needed for their jobs. The ways of working in this routinized and regulated way were minutely described in documents and taught at special sessions. They also prescribed the attitude the employees were to adopt. Everything was to be expressed within the teams where the work was organized, by means of which employer loyalty would be fostered and the desire to find another job reduced.

There were a few carrots connected to this programme: after being trained, each employee was to be rewarded with a discount at a nearby health club as well as very advantageous room rates at the entire chain of hotels. In practice, however, it was a slow process to obtain access to these nice things. There were employees who after two years had still not received their club cards and the hotel rooms turned out to be disappointing. One waiter said: 'you get the smallest and smelliest room that they probably couldn't sell anyway.'

During training, the employees were taught that if they did not perform at a high level, they would be letting the other team members down. The importance of being loyal to the team, being a team player and living up to the responsibilities resting on the team was constantly being impressed on them. But there was a contradiction between all the talk about the team, autonomy and responsibility on the one hand, and the Taylorist practices of the Service Standards on the other. The outcome was that the teams only functioned as teams when their workload was small. When guests came flocking in, such as during the lunch hour or when several coaches arrived at the same time, they did not function at all. In the eyes of the employees, most of the training consisted of rhetoric aimed at fostering loyalty, while practice consisted more of detailed control and an increased workload.

Protests and resistance resulted, both individually and collectively. The meetings that the team leaders arranged to scrutinize the members' performance varied between sullen silences and attacks on management, rather than the team-building and productivity-enhancing exercises they were supposed to be. The carrots were rotten and, to the extent that the workers became team players, they were playing against management rather than for the team in the way management had intended them to.

(Richards and Marks, 2007)

36
The Team Meeting

There was to be a team meeting. For two days, the production manager had been walking around the team's workplace, observing their work and checking the production figures. He had not talked to the workers, only to the management-appointed team leader. It was the team leader's task to act as an intermediary and make sure that management's wishes were realized by the team. He convened a meeting, which for once was to be held upstairs in a room at the offices. Some protests were heard since smoking was prohibited up there, but to no avail. The meeting started and the team leader said they were all welcome to butt in with their comments whenever they wanted.

The business plan for next year was handed out and the team leader started running through it. One of the team members interrupted: 'They tell us what to do, but when are they going to get their asses off their chairs and do something? They get a pay rise and what about us? They don't know what they are doing, they are all idiots they should sort themselves out first.' Without comment, the team leader continued by reading the company mission statement: 'contribute to a better world by developing ourselves and our business activities, in harmony with our environment, thereby creating the opportunity to become respected World Class supplier...' The faces of those in the room were growing more and more tired. The words were as far from the realities of the shop floor as one could get.

The team leader continued with the company's management principles:

- To develop our skills and abilities faster than our competitors
- To improve every aspect of customer service

- To foster teamwork within our organization
- To protect and be sensitive towards the environment

The team members did not recognize their working conditions there either.

The team leader said that ordinary improvement activities were not enough any more: special efforts were needed. Management had made a new plan and formulated a new slogan for the coming year. One of the team members stood up, threw the business plan on the floor and said: 'I've had enough. I'm going to do some work.' Others also started to leave the room. Nobody felt more motivated towards higher efficiency and harder work. Nobody felt that the words of the business plan had anything to do with their work, in spite of their being encouraged to butt in.

(Sharpe, 2006)

37
Trying Again

In the so-called 'new' working life, employees are supposed to be involved in their work and to take responsibility for the results. But at the same time, resources are being reduced within these lean organizations to such an extent that they could rightly be called anorexic. Often, employees have to try to get the resources they need to be able to do their work facing obstacles raised by managers. It has turned out that the employees who are most successful in securing such resources, after having failed once – that is being denied them by a manager – are those who simply keep at it and try again. It pays to nag. It is also the most experienced employees who make that technique to work efficiently. Less experienced employees try to go over their immediate manager's head, but that is a much less successful way, and then they usually give up.

So, if you fail the first time in making your most immediate manager provide you with what you need to get your job done – try again.

(Maslyn, Farmer and Fedor, 1996)

38
The Docile and Loyal Cleaners

This is the story of a Swedish hotel attendant's experiences of her work in a Finnish hotel. It is based on a diary she kept about her work.[1]

My first day as a hotel cleaner. A bit tense, I'm waiting at the reception for my supervisor, Mirka. It's nine in the morning, which is when the cleaners arrive at Mirka's office. She is a blond, tall, bespectacled woman in her forties. I follow her into her office, which is filled with cleaners – all women – from 20 to 60 years old and all dressed in black trousers and wine-coloured shirts. There seems to be a depressed atmosphere in the room and my new workmates look rather bitter and dogged. The hotel is a big international one with four stars; there are eight floors with hotel rooms in long corridors, but our personnel area is at the garage level with a sheet metal floor and gurgling water pipes in the ceiling. The small canteen has no windows and there is toilet paper piled up along one wall.

I can speak my mother tongue, Swedish, with four of the 15 cleaners: Kim, who is also Swedish; Nina, who is a Finland-Swede (for historical reasons there is a Swedish-speaking minority in Finland); and Finnish Hannele and Russian Sofja, who have both learned a bit of Swedish at school. Kim is the cleaner I get the best contact with during my time at the hotel and we even become friends outside work. Most of the cleaners are Finnish, Russian or Estonian. They don't understand each other's language and few have any English. When we try to communicate, it therefore often has to be through sign language, which leads to many misunderstandings. An example is my encounters with Katinka. She is Russian, in her sixties, and her roars echo through the corridors. Several times she shouts at me in Russian and points angrily at her wrist, which I interpret as a fuming call that I should work faster. Therefore I ignore her. After some time I realize, however, that she is not telling me how to do my work, she is only asking what time it is – and the way she does so is in her normal booming tone of voice. Otherwise most cleaners go about their work in silence, looking sour; most of us hardly even greet each other in the mornings.

The most effective cleaner is Russian Tatjana. She is also an informal 'assistant supervisor', who not only rushes in to show others how to clean properly, but also controls our work on instruction from Mirka. It seems that she has to pay for this position by constantly being at the company's disposal, even in the middle of the night. It is also rumoured that management can use her in this way because she would be ordered to leave the country if it were not for this job.

No deeper relations develop across the cultural barriers between us cleaners as our different social and ethnic backgrounds make it difficult for us to find any common denominators. In fact, the ethnic cleavages between us oppose any fellowship and in my clique we even come up with nicknames for some of the other cleaners, such as 'the evil Est', 'Russian robots' or 'the Russian slave' – the latter referring to Tatjana. We also make fun of our occupation and pretend to be proud of our work; for example we photograph each other posing with the vacuum cleaner, faking exaggerated happiness and then publish the pictures on the Internet.

I prefer to associate with people of the same age as me and who also work here temporarily. We share the same views about the work – it is a crappy job with low pay in which management try to change us into cleaning robots – but we know that we will be out of here soon. The older cleaners, especially the Russians and the Estonians, do not have that kind of choice. It is difficult for them to get any other type of job in Finland, so they simply have to try to endure the dreadful working conditions. Still, what we share is that we feel exploited.

The work tasks are simply to clean hotel rooms and sometimes also common areas such as corridors and lifts. The work is lonely as each cleaner has her own work tasks and individual schedule. We do not know the details of the schedule until we get it in the morning and it specifies which rooms to clean and when they are expected to be done. The result is that we finish for the day at different times, depending on our individual schedules and how fast each cleaner is. I often have more than 30 rooms to clean in exactly the same way, which makes the job monotonous and boring. What I dislike most, though, is the stress due to a very pressed time frame: We have maximum 18, preferably 16, minutes to finish a room, regardless of how much work effort every room needs. If I cannot manage each of 'my' rooms in 18 minutes, I have to work longer than the expected time. The pay system is built on an hourly wage, so I get more pay if I work slowly – but then I get punished in other ways.

To have cleaned a room in an approved fashion, the bed or beds must be made; the sheets and the towels must be changed; the floor vacuum-cleaned and washed; glasses, spoons, coffee cups and saucers washed or changed; soaps, shampoos, showering caps, shoeshine, laundry bags, tea- and coffee-bags, toilet paper and information sheets put in place; rubbish and other litter taken away; bathroom cleaned, which includes toilet, shower cabin and floor; tables, mirrors and other surfaces thoroughly polished; missing products from the minibar noted down and replaced; and all furniture neatly put in their predetermined places. Moreover, I have to use a lot of time searching for products for the rooms as they quickly run out in the trolley. Often they are missing even in the storeroom, so I have to go searching in storerooms at other floors. It sometimes feels as if I am spending as much time in the lifts as I put into performing the work itself. Sometimes a room can be exceptionally dirty and therefore needs extra time. It also feels disgusting when the guests have thrown rubbish all over the room and the bed at the same time as all cups and glasses are filled with old dregs. The worst part, though, is when the guests look disdainfully at me while I perform my work – that makes me feel very angry. An example is when I enter a room and there is a businessman there, working at his computer. He does not even move from his chair, which means I have to crawl around his feet to clean the floor. The same man complains to Mirka of my cleaning not being good enough, which results in her ordering me to go back to his room. Since I feel too bad to go there again, I persuade Kim to go in my place.

Management thoroughly controls that we do our work according to the rules and regulations, especially when it comes to time effectiveness. As every cleaner is paid until she has finished 'her' rooms Mirka and other supervisors, including Tatjana, do rounds to make sure that the cleaning is done fast and with high quality. So work is not only to be done fast, but also extremely scrupulously; I often get reprimands from Mirka for having missed some important detail, as for example not arranging a corner of a pillow properly. Once when Kim places an information sign at the wrong side of the TV, Mirka really pours her wrath over her for this mistake. Ultimately, though, cleaning quality does not seem to be as important as working fast. In practice it is what is visible that counts the most – something that can explain why Mirka can become so angry about the sign at the same time as she does not bother to control the minibar.

The knowledge that Mirka sneaks around the corridors forces us to work faster, which is a constant stress. When I meet her in a corridor I find myself walking more quickly so as not to look like I am foot-dragging. Sometimes it happens that another cleaner is sent to me to help me finish on time, which always makes me feel bad as it is a way of saying that I have not done my job properly. The pressure to work against the clock is accentuated by the lack of a lunch break. Formally we have the right to half an hour break for lunch and pay-ment is deducted for that time, but in practice we are not expected to take the break – and few of us do. Initially I try to persuade myself that I have the right to a lunch break and that I do not have to feel ashamed at all – and then I slink away when nobody sees me. During the break I find it difficult to relax, as I keep thinking about all the time lost. Before and after the break I try to work even faster than nor-mal and thereby make it possible to justify taking a lunch break at all. It also feels bad that Mirka can come to control my work anytime – including during lunch time. Whenever I find a note reprimanding me when I return, it feels like she wants to emphasize her displeasure with me being away from work. Soon I stop having lunch.

Almost all cleaners complain about aching shoulders and backs due to the stress and heavy work. We do not make any extra money by stressing and our health suffers, but paradoxically we try to keep up the expected time efficiency. For example, I often meet cleaners *run-ning* between rooms to be able to keep up the demand of 16 minutes per room. Management's main tool to keep up the high work inten-sity is arbitrary individual punishment. For example, when my work tasks have taken too much time, Mirka ignores me when I enter her office at the end of the day, which of course makes me feel terri-ble and gives me a guilty conscience. Other punishments are extra rooms on the schedule and extra days at work when you actually were meant to be free. It also happens that Mirka is doing a cleaner down in front of others.

Apart from the demand of time efficiency, there are also other norms that we have to follow to avoid being punished. For example we cannot express any kind of dissatisfaction or criticism. Kim, who is not always that discrete with her opinions about the job, is denied ending her employment a week before her contract stipulates, even though it turns out to be no problem at all for me to do the same thing. She is also forbidden to listen to music on her MP3 player while working, in spite of both me and other cleaners openly walking around with our earphones without being given a rebuke. The cleaners hide their opposition to avoid being punished, but Kim now and then also shows it more openly in front of Mirka, and for that she is being punished. I do not know whether to call myself a coward or smart, but it seems to benefit me that I am not too open with my dismay. As Mirka and the others do not know my feelings and views, they do not treat me as severely as they do Kim.

The social climate at the workplace is quite closed and the communication between management and us cleaners – apart from orders and abuse from management – is very defective. At the surface this creates docile and loyal cleaners: We work quickly and efficiently, we almost always accept working extra time when management wants us to and I seldom hear anybody express explicit criticism to Mirka. Still, dismay bubbles under the dutiful surface. The bad pay, the brutal work tempo, the constant demands for accessibility, the fact that we do not have any say in anything, and the often inhuman treatment of us does not, however, lead us to protest openly. Further, during my time at the hotel I am never contacted by any representative of a trade union, in fact I never hear anyone mention the existence of a union.

To fiddle with the cleaning is a must if I am to manage to finish a hotel room within the time frame of 16 to 18 minutes. As the company does not welcome criticism and suggestions on the cleaners' part, we simply solve the problem of time by cheating through not cleaning as scrupulously as we could. In this we always take risks, as we break management's strict directives of accuracy and are liable to be reprimanded and have to do it over again if we get caught. It is a constant struggle between our fiddling and management's control of our job. With time I learn small tricks, how to cheat with neither Mirka nor the guests noticing. The most important thing is to clean what can be seen. I do not bother about washing the floor if it looks fairly clean. Instead of polishing with a dust cloth I quickly draw the feather duster over paintings, tables and desks. It is also sometimes possible not to check and fill the minibar, as the guests usually are not aware of what is supposed to be in there anyway. Occasionally a guest has had a meal in the room, which leaves a tray and dirty dishes. I never understand whether it is my responsibility to take care of the tray, nobody has ever informed me about that either, but as I suspect that it in fact *is* my responsibility I secretly put it in the store room and then I have no idea how it got there. The best time-gaining trick is to refrain from changing the bed sheets when a new guest is arriving, although it is possible only if they still look fresh and are not too crumpled. The changing of sheets and making of the bed is the most time-consuming and heavy work task and when I can get away with not doing that it is a real victory.

Thefts are quite common among the cleaners. Equipment and supplies disappear without a trace. We have two trolleys at each floor which we have to share with one another. We can fill them with for example soaps to last us for the day, but after only a few hours we have to fill it up again. Nobody talks about this or lets on that it is strange, but we are all well aware of what is going on. Apart from hygiene supplies and other small things like tea bags, shower caps, sewing- and tooth brush kits, which seem to disappear at a rapid pace, thefts of a bit bigger type occurs. It happens that hotel guests forget private things in the rooms and we cleaners are supposed to hand them in at the office, but that does not always happen. Also products from the minibar, not only chocolate and crisps but also spirits, tend to disappear quickly. When it comes to alcohol I only dare to steal two mini-bottles of vodka during my whole time at the hotel – and I go to another floor, pretending to fetch more tea bags, in order to do so. Kim steals more than I do. At one occasion in her apartment she shows me two crammed drawers with the results of her raids, which include working clothes and toilet paper. Apart from useful goods she steals things like 'Do not disturb'-signs and 'Pillow menu'-signs. The main point, she says, is not to get hold of the things as such but the *action* in itself. She takes something home every day and thinks it is rewarding that she can get away with it. The thefts become a positive trait of our working day as we get something else than the boring work tasks to think about. Stealing has become a game and through it we have found some meaning in work. Not once do Kim or I feel that we are doing something morally wrong – rather our bitterness at our working conditions justifies more thefts. Considering all stress and hard work we think we actually deserve some free soap.

On the rare occasions when I have a bit of time over before the set finishing time, for example when I happen to have relatively clean rooms, I do not want to go to the office right away. If I do I either have to help someone else or go home, which means that I do not get more pay that day. Instead I clean really slowly or I stay in a room just to breathe a few minutes. Sometimes I combine the rest with eating stolen chocolate. I also see other cleaners talking in their mobiles quite often and sending text messages. I regard these occasions as possibilities to take back time and energy that we give away all the time, but never get properly compensated for by the greedy hotel. Still, there is always the risk of being found out, as Mirka can walk into any room anytime.

(Lundberg and Karlsson, 2011)

39
Compensating

A barmaid asked the catering manager if she could leave 15 minutes early to catch a bus, otherwise she would have to wait for the 3 a.m. bus, not getting home until 4 a.m. She then had to get up at 7 a.m. to get her kids off to school, but the manager refused to let her go. She tried to persuade him, but he just said that it was his decision and he did not feel like letting her go. The barmaid went back to work thinking: 'The only way to get home in time is to take a taxi, and he is going to pay for it.' With the help of a workmate, she succeeded in pilfering enough money from the cash register to cover the taxi fare.

There was also an informal rate among the employees regarding how much they could steal to compensate for their low wages and bad treatment. This was regarded as fair. One of them said:

> The irony of it all is that not only are we not paid enough for what we do here, we are also compelled to pilfer a fraction of what's rightfully ours. On top of that we're expected to feel guilty and ashamed of what we have done, what a laugh…(36)

The managers also compensated themselves for being badly treated by managers higher up in the hierarchy by stealing, and in other ways. In cases like that, much greater assets were at stake as they had access to quite different types of resources.

(Analoui and Kakabadse, 1989)

40
One Minute

All movements were calculated in units of less than seconds. In the afternoons, the line was stopped for ten minutes for a break. But this time, it had been started up after only nine minutes. Massive dismay: 'It is not time yet! One minute left!' But everyone started work at once because they did not want to fall behind at their stations. However, their fury became stronger and stronger. Robbed of a whole minute! Finally, some of the bravest workers switched off the power and the line stopped. The supervisors came running in and it took them a minute to get the line going again. The workers felt very refreshed at having recaptured their minute. Some smiles were even to be seen along the line.

(Linhart, 1978)

41
Tackling Time

Work at this industrialized, conveyor-belt bakery is very dull and humdrum, heavy and hot. There are wall clocks everywhere, but 'it seems like there's some bugger standing on the hands of the clock and stopping them going round', one of the workers often puts it. Some of the jobs are fairly comfortable – they could be learned by anyone in a few seconds and they do not require any attentiveness on the part of the worker – but nobody wants them; they are too boring. Instead, they all want jobs that demand something of them, in spite of being heavier and hotter. There are even degrees of monotony.

To get by in this environment, the workers have invented different ways of exerting an influence on time. It is not piecework, so they cannot amuse themselves by finding angels in order to fix the piece rate. The wage system is based on being paid by the hour, so what they can do is tackle time itself. One way is to 'make time'. Officially, there are two 15-minute tea-breaks during each shift, but there are ways of making more time for breaks. One way is quite simple: the clocks show slightly different times, making it possible to start a break by a fast clock and come back by a slow one, and in doing so gain a few minutes. A more complicated method is to work in such a way that a 'natural gap' is created at the beginning of the process. This can be made big enough to accommodate a cigarette or a cup of tea. It also gradually moves down the production line, making it possible for other workers to enjoy it.

Another possibility is 'counting time twice' – that is, getting paid for time when one is not actually working. Engineers have calculated that a certain kind of bread takes 27.5 minutes to bake. The working time for a shift is arranged in such a way that a certain number of batches can be produced; however, in practice, this time can vary slightly. Therefore, each shift is paid for each extra 15 minutes, counting backwards. This benefits the workers if the last batch is finished in exactly 15 minutes, or only a few minutes into a new quarter of an hour. If it takes 13 or 14 minutes into a new quarter of an hour, they will not be paid for that time. If the batch is threatening to finish at a time that is unfavourable to the workers, the oven can, however, be operated faster or slower to make the batch fit better into the 15-minute cycle. In that way, the workers can gain earnings for each of the shifts of up to 15 minutes extra, instead of losing pay for up to 15 minutes. (This is a much simplified description. In reality, these manipulations of time are considerably more complicated, including combinations of speeding up and slowing down the process.) The effect can also be augmented by letting all but one on the shift go and the remaining worker then clocks out for the whole shift.

A third way is to 'arrest time', which means stopping the conveyor belt. The result is a break that can alleviate the monotony a bit. This can be done by being negligent as regards maintenance, or by direct sabotage. At a smaller oven, finally, there is something called the 'negotiation of time'. The calculated time for a certain kind of bread is 8.5 minutes, while for another it is 32.5. The shorter time makes work stressful, while the longer makes it tedious. During periods of strong sales, the workers can informally negotiate the possibility of prolonging the first time period and shortening the second by a few minutes. This reduces the quality of the bread, but it makes life a bit easier for the bakery workers.

(Ditton, 1979)

42
The Broken Bar Shutters

When the bars of the nightclub closed, heavy shutters had to be pulled down. They were old and did not function very well, so there were often near-accidents and the staff were constantly complaining about the risks. In spite of that management refused to have them renovated or replaced. The cost would be astronomical, they said. But when two customers were injured by the shutters, new ones were finally installed. The general manager called a meeting, pointed to the shutters and declared: 'Those shutters cost 1000 quid, more than all of you lot are worth. I can replace you lot anytime I wish, but I can't afford those shutters again. Make sure that they're not dropped on the counters.'

The staff who had nagged so much about getting new shutters now pulled them with such force that they soon became useless. 'If the shutters are worth more than me (workers) do you wonder how much exactly we are each worth... down with the shutters...' one of them exclaimed.

(Analoui and Kakabadse, 1989)

43
The Kettle

A group of skilled setters were responsible for setting up automatic lathes. Often it took a long time to adjust the feeds and speeds, but when they had achieved the correct settings, the machines could run with very little human intervention. The engineering department had decided on norms for the settings, but the group set the speeds higher – although not so high as to jeopardize safety. The setters had prepared a room close by where they had installed a kettle to make tea. When the machines were set up the way they wanted, the workers sat there having tea and listening to the machines. Any change in the sound meant that something needed to be adjusted.

Management did not like the group just sitting there, seemingly without doing any work. One morning, when the workers arrived, they discovered that the socket for their kettle had been disconnected. Without comment, they started having their tea and lunch breaks in the canteen. During that time, they shut the machines down, which was exactly what the rule book said they should do. And during working hours, they slowed the machines down to the speed they should be run at according to the engineering department. After only a few days, the power was reconnected and they could use the kettle and room once again. They returned to setting the machines at the speed they decided themselves, not the one recommended by the engineering department, and management stopped bothering them.

(White, 1988)

44
Many Glasses

This nightclub was so big that there were special staff, 'glass collectors', who picked up used glasses and carried them to the bar staff, who then washed and stacked them. When management talked about co-operation, they meant unconditional obedience to what managers said. The glass collectors had, however, their own ways of co-operating to make the work flow – ways that they defended when threatened by management. When a new supervisor was appointed, the catering manager told the glass collectors that they had to cooperate with him or else they would be fired. That weekend, the bar was stacked so full of glasses that the bar staff had no chance of doing much more than washing and stacking them. The guests had to wait to be served and started complaining.

One of the directors happened to be at the club and noticed what was going on. He told the catering manager off, wondering if he really was able to manage his staff. A little later, the glass collectors were called in to the catering manager, who said: 'You know the best way to do it so I will leave you to it.'

(Analoui and Kakabadse, 1989)

45
The Informal Rules

In a US factory in the 1930s, these informal rules were in force among the workers:

- You should not turn out too much work. If you do you are a rate buster.
- You should not turn out too little work. If you do you are a chiseller.
- You should not tell a supervisor anything that will react to the detriment of an associate. If you do you are a squealer.
- You should not attempt to maintain social distance or act officious. If you are an inspector, for example, you should not act like one (522).

The same informal rules were in force among the workers at a Norwegian factory in the 1950s, and they were still there in 2007.

(Roethlisberger and Dickson, 1965 [1939]; see also Lysgaard, 2001 [1961] and Hansen, 2007)

46
The Academics' Real Work

Academics are hardly known for resistance in the workplace. They are, perhaps, better known for constant intrigues regarding career steps and research grants. But, possibly, something is happening. The background is a trend towards managerialism, which means that universities are now being managed like any other organization. Academics are also being burdened with growing administrative tasks: forms to fill in, bureaucratic reports to write and send to some or other manager, and administrative meetings they are expected to participate in. This involves market orientation and a great stress on economic considerations. Managers get more say – teachers and researchers less.

But to the academics, these growing administrative tasks are not their real work. Their workload has gradually grown, but the part of it constituting research has shrunk. At the same time, they are protecting their real work – research – from infringement using all means at their disposal. They regard research to be an exiting, creative and engaging activity, and something they want to do. It is their own activity; everything else is a burden dumped on them from above, preventing them from performing their real work. This way of looking at research means that working time becomes a very diffuse concept. It is impossible to say that it starts at 7 a.m. and ends at 4 p.m. All time is potential working time, including holidays, nights and weekends.[1] And research is more and more being forced away from normal working hours since that is when most administrative duties have to be performed.

When the university sent an associate lecturer a 20-page survey to fill in, he instead wrote a letter to the manager responsible. He wrote that the survey was much too long, that many of the questions were stupid and that it was 'slightly insulting' to believe that he would have time to fill it in. Otherwise, a common tactic is to simply ignore everything that comes from admin for the time being – and throw everything away for which there has not yet been a reminder. Besides, many can allude to the absent-minded professor cliché, saying that they had simply forgotten that there was a note that they were supposed to read and new regulations that they were supposed to follow.

Not just time but also space can be mobilized in order to defend research against the new managerialism. To a higher and higher degree, academics are leaving their university offices – offices where they feel disturbed, interrupted and forced to perform irrelevant tasks. Instead, they stay at home in order to be able to do their real work. For example, an associate professor received an e-mail from a deputy vice-chancellor containing complaints that certain academics could seldom be found in their offices. He answered: 'Look, if you ever find me in my office, I'm not doing my job.' He added that on the last two occasions when he had been looking for the deputy vice-chancellor, she had not been in her room.

Academics' resistance consists of doing their real work. That is the source of their dignity.

(Anderson, 2006, 2008)

47
Machines, Pieces of Paper and Rubber Bands

Fifteen years ago, management bought used machines and these have never functioned properly. When workers are hired, they have to sign a document saying that if they break the house rules, they will be dismissed. One of the rules is that they always have to call in the maintenance department if a problem arises with a machine. In spite of that, they take care of the constantly jammed machines themselves as they do not think that the maintenance department is competent enough to do so. One of them said: 'Maintenance don't know shit about this machine. You gotta be able to fix it. Sure they know how to replace something but they really don't know how it works.' The machines have to run properly if the flow of work is to be maintained.

Since the workers are breaching the rules whenever they repair the machines, they have to conceal what they do from management. The result is that they do not have access to the tools and materials necessary to do this work, instead having to use whatever they can get their hands on: pieces of paper and rubber bands, for example.

(Martin, 1986)

48
Combing One's Hair

There were many rules. The workers were not allowed to loiter on the stairs, in the corridors, in the entrances. They were not allowed to go to other toilets than those intended for them. Their clothes and bags could be searched at any time, to prevent them from stealing. All these rules were constantly being propagated by management, and there were also notices, making the workers feel as though they were back at school. There was, however, one rule that they accepted as rational: 'The combing of hair is forbidden in any Department.' Loose hairs could get into the product and, although they regarded breaking the rules as a symbol of autonomy, they did not want a low-quality product.

One day, management was visited by some important guests, who were shown around the workplace. The event was to be immortalized in photographs. The photographer arranged the visitors and managers into photographable positions and prepared his camera. To look good, the visitors took out combs and started to comb their hair. The managers did not say anything about this being prohibited, instead combing their hair too. A couple of the workers started to shout at the most senior manager: 'He's combing his hair! If we combed our hair in the factory, he'd go out of his mind.' 'Well, that's nice, he ought to practice what he preaches.' But the managers and the visitors just carried on with their grooming.

(Pollert, 1981)

49
How to Get Rid of a Critic

If a critic from the lower rungs of an organization seems to articulate what many feel, and also presents solutions to problems, there are four successive steps whereby managers can act in order to intimidate them into submission. Management's goal is partly to control the critic so that they do not obtain a following and partly to enact this control in such a way that management cannot be blamed for anything.

The first of these steps is nullification. Management tries to convince the critic that their accusations and suggestions are groundless. They have misunderstood everything, from start to finish. But if they continue not to acquiesce, management will offer to appoint a committee, which will investigate the question thoroughly. Management will say: 'You don't know what you're talking about, but thank you anyway for telling us. We'll certainly look into the matter for you.' Then the question will be buried by the committee.

If this information does not silence the critic, the second step is isolation. The critic is separated from their peers, superiors and subordinates, if any, making it impossible for them to mobilize support and a following. They can, for example, be transferred to another post with fewer organizational resources. The managers say: 'If you insist on talking about things which you do not understand, then we will have to prevent you from bothering other people with your nonsense.' The critic will be taught not to try to initiate change, but to wait until change is requested by management.

Defamation is the third step, and is taken if the critic – in spite of management's striving against it – succeeds in mobilizing support for their position. Nasty rumours are suddenly spread at the workplace regarding the personality and character of the critic. Their motives are dubious; they are disgustingly incompetent, or probably mentally ill. The message is: 'Don't listen to them, because you can't trust a person like them.' The idea is to focus attention on the critic, not on the problem or those responsible for it. In doing which, the way is paved for the last step.

If defamation fails, there will only be one option left: expulsion. Preferably, the critic should withdraw from the organization of their own free will: 'Give notice yourself and you will not be denounced as having been sacked.'

(O'Day, 1974)

50
The Seagull Managers

A nurse says this about the managers at the hospital where she works: 'We have seagull managers here, they fly in from a great height, make a lot of noise, drop a lot of crap, then they fly off again.'

(Cooke, 2006)

51
Live Time, Wrap Time and Idle Time

The employees who remained after the restructuring of the bank did two types of tasks. One was to answer phone calls from customers, the other to process other matters. Work was organized in teams with team leaders appointed by managers higher up in the hierarchy. The team members had to work the phone lines for two 2-hour periods a day, but they were also expected to step in if the call backlog became too long. The direct contact with the customer was called 'live time' and could not be longer than 20 seconds per call. If the employee had to check out the answers to questions, then they would have to make a note and finish the call. The time it took to make the note was known as the 'wrap time' and they could not deal with queries until after their phone session. The live time had to be maximized and was the measurement of productivity. Time spent visiting the toilet or having a coffee-break was not, as one might think, called dead time but instead 'idle time'. At present, the bank was trying to diminish the wrap time because it reduced productivity. The measurement of productivity had nothing to do with the quality of the service but was purely quantitative: the time an employee spent answering calls divided by the number of incoming calls.

The time pressure when answering phone calls caused a lot of stress, as did shifting between that and other tasks. The computer system added to the stress. It calculated how many employees had to man the phones at different points in time, being programmed not to take staff absence into account. If someone was absent, the other employees had to cover for them.

The number of employees reporting in sick was on the increase and management's countermove was to intensify the level of control. The following discussion took place during a team meeting:

> *Team leader*: As you know we have to ring in sick, and we're going to have a register so that when senior management come down, and ask why there are backlogs, then we can explain.
> *Staff*: It's all the stress.
> *Team leader*: We the green team have the worst sickness, it's at 11 per cent...In the future, all complaints will be logged, and it means that we'll have to deal with less crap because we can go back to who did it ... If we can get rid of that backlog next week it would be wonderful. (178–9, emphasis removed)

The comment about stress was totally neglected by the team leader. Instead of commenting on it, she emphasizes that 'we' will be able to identify the guilty people through the individual registering of cases of sickness. This is, of course, a veiled threat against the team members and an exhortation not to call in sick. The stress that the employees express is nothing worth talking about, only the responsibility to senior management for productivity.

Thus, it was up to the employees to handle their working conditions in unofficial ways to reduce the stress. They had to find cracks in management's control that they could then use. One way was to pretend to be talking to a customer by phone. They would put on their headsets and move their lips as though talking to someone, but they had not logged on a call and so could enjoy a 20-second break. Another way was to cut the customer off if the call threatened to be longer than the stipulated time, or if it was an unusually annoying customer. A further reason to do this was if a worker was having trouble with productivity figures: if the call finished during the live time, the numbers would be positive and no wrap time would be registered. It was a different issue that this provided the customer with poor service – that was not part of the measurement.

(Knights and McCabe, 1998)

52
The Being Yourself Culture

The managers said that they all respected the fact that the Telephone Sales Agents at the airline knew better than anyone how to do their jobs: they knew what their customers wanted and they knew how to sell. They all agreed, management said, that the goal was for as many phone calls as possible to result in actual bookings and sales of travel-related services. Just be yourselves, management said. We'll give you the time to build up a rapport with your customers – then you'll be successful at selling services. Some customers want to chat about this and that when booking their trips. The culture here empowers you to talk a bit extra. We trust you.

However, at the same time, management was keen on training all Telephone Sales Agents in how to behave and, in particular, which feelings to display to the customer. In these cases, all the talk about being yourself was forgotten in favour of learning how to behave in ways that management thought would increase sales. If, for example, you were dealing with an unusually morose and unpleasant customer, you would absolutely not be allowed to be unpleasant yourself – you had to think that something terrible had happened to this person to make them behave like that. This customer had to be pitied; I have to help them – that was the way to see it.

Furthermore, every Telephone Sales Agent was subject to an extensive and advanced control system. Managers could listen in on and tape any phone call without the prior knowledge of the agent in question. It was also common that a sales team supervisor would simply sit down behind an agent, listen in on their calls and take notes regarding any mistakes that were made. The Telephone Sales Agents could even be forced to record their own calls and hand over the tapes to the sales team supervisor to be evaluated. Each of them also had a personal productivity goal, which they were expected to sur-pass each month. The computer system measured the number of calls each seller made per week, the duration of each call and how long the pauses were between calls. Every Telephone Sales Agent was assigned goals in all these respects. Everything was then put together and the agent's salary was determined according to their results.

However, the agents had ways of knowing whether they were being listened in on or being physically or electronically supervised. They all sat in an open-plan office – called a community – and it was a sign that you were being monitored if a sales team supervisor cast a furtive glance at you every now and then. When someone was convinced they were not being listened in on, they could do what management claimed the company culture offered: being (at least more) themselves. 'When she [the supervisor] is not listening, I just prefer to be myself...when I am positive she is not listening, I have been really short with bad customers, it's a great feeling,' said one of them. At times like these, calls from difficult customers could sud-denly be interrupted for inexplicable reasons. In ways like these, the Telephone Sales Agents were sometimes able to empower themselves.

(Taylor, 1998)

53
The Employees Who Wanted to Be Taped

The rules at Holidayco said that all staff in contact with customers by phone were to be monitored frequently by means of taping calls. By doing this, deficiencies could be corrected and the number of served customers could increase. Every taped call was to be played back to the employee and then discussed with the team leader, which would result in identifying areas needing to be improved. But at this local office, managers and team leaders thought that those were much too time-consuming tasks – arranging the recording, listening to the tape, letting the sales agent listen to it and then discussing what was said. 'We have more important things to do,' they felt. Officially, they claimed that the taping of calls was routine at the office; however, if it had been left up to local management, not much would have been taped and monitored.

The lack of taping, however, sometimes resulted in the agents requesting to be recorded. Instead of the aim of monitoring being to control or discipline them, they started to use it as a resource for themselves. They had two reasons for this. The first goal superficially resembled the one set by the head office with regard to the monitoring, but was different in reality. Both wanted to improve work, but by improving, they meant different things. Senior management wanted to increase the number of calls each sales agent took in order to improve profits; it strove for enhanced quantity. The agents, however, wanted to improve the quality of their contact with the customers. People called the travel agency for positive experiences gained through rewarding journeys – something towards which the employees wanted to contribute. By listening to their own calls now and then, they hoped to be able to improve their con-tribution towards good travel experiences. The other reason was to protect themselves against accusations of treating customers badly. When they had a 'difficult call' – an angry customer who shouted and screamed and threatened to report them to management – they gave a sign that they wanted to be recorded. If they were reported, they would thus be able to prove that they had behaved politely and correctly towards the customer.

The superiors at the local branch misbehaved organizationally in relation to company rules concerning the taping of the sales agents' customer calls, but this opened up the possibility of the sellers taking over this technology as a resource in their work.

(Lankshear et al., 2001)

54
When Management Lets Go

When workplaces are closed down, management often releases its grip on production, allowing productivity rise. Before the decision is definite, frustration, stress and anger prevail among the employees. Work motivation drops, as does productivity. Protests and resistance grow. But when it becomes clear that there will be a close-down, the trend reverses. The workers want to show management that it has made a great mistake and resistance ceases: they do not hold back on their labour power anymore and productivity starts to rise. This goes on for a while, but soon the workers find that this display of additional endeavour is of very little help. The close-down still stands.

Now, however, management cares less and less about work on the shop floor. Managers have other things to see to – and besides, this workplace will soon be gone. In step with control from above loosening, worker self-control grows. They form other teams based on their own principles, they take initiatives of their own for improvements to production, and they rationalize the production process. Instead of using their creativity for resistance, they put it into their work. As management has let go, there is nothing to resist anymore, nobody to misbehave against. Productivity keeps increasing – until the workplace no longer exists.

(Bergman and Wigblad, 1999; Hansson, 2008)

55
Call Centre Vocabulary

At an Irish call centre, there is a whole vocabulary among the employees regarding measures taken against dignity-threatening working conditions: slammin', scammin', smokin' and leavin'. Slammin' takes place while on the phone. Bonuses are an important part of earnings, making it vital to register as many sales as possible. When sales are slow and the workers only reach answering machines, they can go on as usual and pretend that they are talking to a customer and then put the call down as a sale. They think it is all right to do this as they constantly feel cheated by management:

> Well, you can understand why we would want to earn the money in any way we can. After all they promised £5.00 an hour going up to £6.00, and bonuses. But we never got more than £4.50, because they always found a reason why you didn't make the grade. So if someone was doing it, and they were, I mean, I'd say, 'It's alright'. (715)

But slammin' also has a wider meaning, namely distancing yourself from and taking a cynical attitude towards the corporate culture that management works so hard to impose on the employees.

Scammin' is work avoidance and absenteeism. There is great pressure from management not to be absent from work; for example, through a 'back to work interview' that each employee who has been off sick has to undergo. Management also tries to induce the teams to put pressure on workers not to be absent. But scammin' becomes a little bit easier when team members refuse to do this. They regard being absent from time to time as a necessity in order to be able to put up with the job.

Smokin' is not just for smokers – the term refers to short meetings during extra breaks to discuss some specific aspect of working conditions and what can be done. Smokin' is, then, an expression of a collectivity that goes beyond the collectivism that management tries to put in place through the teams being organized from above.

Leavin' means, of course, quitting the job. When no other means of keeping your dignity remain, you leave – if you can. At this call centre, working conditions are bad and labour turnover is high. One former employee tells this story:

> It was a struggle for me to get to the end of the week, I got very stressed and would crash out. Just being away from the place was great, then you walk in on Monday and it starts all over again. I couldn't cope with this see-saw life and left.

Leavin' also inspires others to leave: 'It puts pressure on others more than you can imagine. It gets so bad with so many people leavin'. Fourteen left in one swoop last week.'

Slammin', scammin', smokin' and leavin' – the vocabulary that Irish call centre workers use when resisting undignified working conditions.

(Mulholland, 2004)

56
The Dress Code

A dress code was issued at the office decreeing that all employees must wear a shirt and tie. Many thought it uncomfortable and everyone thought that this was expensive. There were quiet conferences by the water cooler and behind closed doors.

The next morning, the office was filled with the most awful combinations of loathsome ties and glaringly colourful shirts. One of the employees said of his dress: 'I wore a tie about four or five inches wide, illustrating the history and future of the motor car in glorious technicolour, along with a purple-checked shirt.' The written record does not tell what happened next, but one of the authors has told me that management withdrew the dress code the very next day.

(Taylor and Bain, 2003, 2004)

57
Promises, Customer Service and Profit

The clerical workers thought they were doing an important job, and they were proud of serving the customers of this privatized utility so well. Management regarded the employees as 'very accommodating', but said that some changes would have to be made in order to serve the customers even better. Thus, the clerical workers' duties would be enriched and contain more opportunities for personal development.

In practice, management concentrated on two points. One was to intensify work and the other was to adjust the number of employees to the variations in the workload. The strategy used to achieve these goals was to fragment, standardize and simplify their tasks, centralize the control that the clerks had previously had over planning and working pace, and reduce the firm's dependence on the individual employee's knowledge and experience. The instruments used to do this included, on the one hand, a new computer system and, on the other, creating work teams made up of clerical workers with insecure employment. With the help of the computer system, management reached fragmentation and simplification by means of much of the necessary knowledge being entered into the computers. What could be routinized was constantly being routinized. In so doing, the simplified work processes could be organized in teams and intensified. As so much occupational skill was removed from the job, management could also cut down on staffing levels and hiring part-time workers.

Management's claims that all changes were aimed at improving customer service resulted in the clerical workers initially viewing these in a positive light. However, they grew more and more suspicious. Right from the start, the computer system caused a lot of trouble. Instead of functioning as a work aid, it brought about the extensive duplication of tasks. The system did not always manage to register information that was to be registered, which meant that clerical staff had to keep records on paper to which corrections and additions were made. Things went so far that new employees had to be hired to help take care of all the problems that the system was causing. One of the clerks said: 'We have customers phoning in complaining all the time...we want to give them a good service, but we can't, and we're the ones taking all the flak.' Another commented: 'The main thing about these new systems is that they make work so frustrating. They were designed "up there"...Management didn't come down to grass-roots and ask us what our jobs entailed, what problems needed to be got round.' Despite the problems, management said it would be too expensive to modify the system more than once a year, which resulted in further problems for the employees: backlogs grew, as did the number of complaining customers. This led to the clerical staff becoming more dissatisfied, especially as management had claimed that it was to achieve better service that the changes were made in the first place.

The office workers talked more and more often about how management wanted to implement the reorganization 'on the cheap', without any training costs and too few employees to get the job done. The service provided to the customers was already suffering from understaffing, and the clerical staff were not being compensated in any way for their intensified workloads and their less secure employment situation. On top of that, the trouble with the computer system showed that the employees had skills that had not been noticed before. The system could at best handle routine tasks but, when problems and critical situations arose, the skills of the clerical staff were needed for the work to get done. 'I don't think we realized before just how much management depends on us knowing about the job,' was one comment.

More and more, it appeared as though management and the office workers had conflicting interests, especially as permanent full-time employment was being replaced by part-time temporary contracts. One of the clerks pondered: 'I used to think that managers and staff were part of a team, but with the new systems coming in it is very much like being on opposing sides.' This feeling was nurtured by the chasm between management's talk about the importance of good service and the lack of resources to provide just that. The employees became convinced that, in practice, the customers were not very important; instead, it was profit that was decisive for management. Profit was the reason for management's empty promises, which made the clerical staff the target of customer hostility on a daily basis.

Resistance to the bad working conditions, and being forced by management to reduce the level of service, both started to materialize. Several cases of sabotage occurred; for example, overloading the computer system with the result that information disappeared. Walk-outs also occurred during the busiest parts of the day. Many of the employees wanted to leave the firm and find another job, but there were no such opportunities, or very few. The existence of this resistance was really remarkable as these were employees who had recently been so proud of their capacity to provide good service in an important job. Empty promises, losing the prerequisites for providing service and having profit as the most important goal had all gradually changed their way of thinking and acting.

The organizational misbehaviour of the clerical staff did not, however, succeed in preventing the deterioration of their working conditions, only in delaying it. A strong group of managers, on a labour market that was quite favourable to employers, succeeded in having things their way in spite of the resistance.

(O'Connell Davidson, 1994)

58
Food for Stable Staff

Stable staff – stable lads and lasses – are employed at small companies owned by horse trainers and their job is to take care of racehorses and prepare them for races. Often, trainers and stable staff work together, making them easy to supervise. At the same time, the lads and lasses develop strong emotional ties with their horses and, if they work hard and efficiently, they may even be allowed to ride them in races. Together, all of this makes resistance unusual and, when it occurs, it mainly takes individual forms. There is a union, but it is weak and there is great pressure on stable staff not to join it. A couple of comments: 'We can't join a union, that would harm the horses' and 'Joining a union? You'd be regarded as a traitor.'

But on one occasion in the English racing town of Newmarket, the stable staff found that they could not get into the staff canteen because members of the public had been allowed in and were filling it. The problem was not only that they could not get food but also that the canteen was an important meeting place for exchanging stories about employers and employment conditions. The stable staff were used to a diet of both meals and information at the canteen, but now they were bereft of both. Nobody took any notice of their complaints. Somehow, a horse lorry happened to break down outside the canteen, blocking the road. Soon about 30 lorries, with at least as many horses, were queuing. The horses could not be offloaded and the start of the race was getting closer. It did not take long before members of the public were referred to the other restaurants and the stable staff were able to get both kinds of sustenance in their canteen again.

(Winters, 2008)

59
The Diagram

The organizational development consultant had brought along a diagram of employee reactions to organizational change. It is a bell curve, he said, '10 per cent are enthusiastic, 80 per cent are generally followers, and 10 per cent actively resist'. One of the shop floor operators protested: 'The diagram is fine, but it is more like 90 per cent who will actively resist!'

(Badham et al., 2003)

60
Allen Smithee

When Hollywood film directors found they had lost creative control over their films due to interventions on the part of the film studios, they started to protest by refusing to be credited as directors. Instead, they all used the fictitious name Allen Smithee. Until now, a lot of films, TV episodes and music videos have officially been directed by Alan Smithee – so many that a new pseudonym has been introduced: Thomas Lee. Do not see their films.

(Braddock and Hock, 2001)

61
Monitoring Creative Employees

An American phone company secretly installed equipment to monitor work, but the employees found out. Soon, management noticed that it was not getting the information it had expected – the employees had created ways of manipulating the monitoring system. One manager commented:

> I cannot begin to tell you about the agitation that was caused, or the creativity which went into beating the system. You got to love folks for that kind of ingenuity. We had one heck of a protest.

> It came from the hurt. That's what made them so sad and angry: feeling that they were being shut out and spied upon, with no say-so whatsoever, because they couldn't be trusted. (89)

Not all managers are as clear-sighted as this one.

(Hornstein, 1996)

62
A Heroine

The office was to be computerized; computers were delivered but, for the time being, they were stored in the cellar. Soon afterwards, some water pipes burst, the cellar flooded and the computers were destroyed. Initially, the event was regarded as an accident, but soon a rumour spread that one of the employees had consciously sabotaged the pipes in order to obstruct computerization. It did not take long before a certain employee, a woman, was singled out as the culprit. The managers and the employees were all convinced of this.

This woman had been a severe critic of management for a long time. She had warned that computerization could result in redundancies and that those remaining could encounter health problems. Even earlier, she had been regarded as troublesome in the eyes of management, but she was respected by her fellow employees for her boldness. However, she pretended not to notice the rumours calling her a saboteur and she never mentioned the incident – something that further added to the belief that she was responsible for the pipes bursting.

Since management thought she was a troublemaker, and now a saboteur, it very much wanted to fire her. However, this was impossible as it was only a rumour and there was no evidence. Among the employees, she increasingly took on the aura of a heroine. The workplace needed, they thought, someone who could stand up to management. By showing that the workers could react to management's power, she had strengthened the positions of all the other workers. Management must not feel too sure that something unpleasant would never happen again.

It never became clear whether it was an accident or sabotage, but a heroine had emerged. In parts of today's management theory, it is stressed that it is important for managers to become heroes in the eyes of the employees. However, this was another type of hero; an employee-heroine standing up to management.

(Prasad and Prasad, 2000, 2001)

63
Giving Face

In China, any questioning of a manager by workers means that the manager loses face. It is important to 'have face' and a manager gets face from their workers. Workers can decide if they want to 'give face' or not. This brings drama to something that to us can seem rather trivial events. An example of this is a controversy between the assistant workshop director, Mr Shen, and the crane operator, Mr Zhou. Mr Shen ordered Mr Zhou to move some parts to another place in the workshop, but Mr Zhou said that it would be better to do it later, when all the parts had arrived. Mr Shen became very upset, not so much because Mr Zhou did not carry out the order immediately but because several other workers were present and – even worse – a researcher witnessed what happened. Mr Shen felt that he had lost face; he then became flushed and exclaimed: 'No wonder other people say that we have too many crane operators over here!' This was a rather concrete threat to Mr Zhou as the labour market was very difficult, and there was a lot of joblessness.

Usually, however, managers try to avoid direct confrontation with their workers, because the risk of losing face is great. This gives rise to advanced inventiveness on both sides when it comes to finding ways of keeping one's dignity. Here is an example. At one workplace, there was a system of fines for workers who made mistakes or committed breaches of discipline. Senior management tightened up the rules and demanded that every workshop director impose 100 fines per month. Those that did not reach this quota would be fined themselves. The intention was to increase management control over the labour process. But the workers and several junior managers thought this was an unusually stupid idea: how could there be exactly 100 such crimes each month? And if there were not, would the workshop directors then have to invent them?

The workshop director, Mr Wang, was among those who did not like the new regulation at all. He had to find a way of giving his superiors what they wanted without provoking his subordinates. He made it clear to the workers that the rule came from above and that he thought it was unfair but that he could not get rid of it. In secrecy, however, he developed a system in order to get round the rule: workers who were fined received an equivalent weighting in their bonus. Soon, the workers got the idea and said among themselves that they did not have to worry about the new rule – in one way or another, Mr Wang would make sure that they got their money back. Workers even offered to be fined if Mr Wang was having trouble reaching the quota. They gave him face.

In this way, Mr Wang succeeded in keeping up appearances as regards sticking to senior management's regulation while at the same time avoiding loss of face in relation to his workers.

(Zhang, 2008)

64
Hot-Desking and Family Photos

'Hot-desking' is when an office employee does not have a desk of their own: on arriving at work, the employee has to grab any desk available. Employers, management and consultants call it the 'non-territorial office'. This renders impossible what most people working in offices want: making a corner of the workplace feel as if it has some personal significance to them. This is done in rather simple terms, such as placing a photo of your loved ones on the desk, or putting up a comic strip that makes a statement about what you regard to be important in your life or a picture that you think is beautiful and inspires you.

An employee in a hot-desking office wanted to keep her personal dignity and put up more photos and posters than was allowed. She was severely punished by management. Word of the incident spread all over the workplace. Soon, family photos and posters were hanging in abundance above the workstations in the office. The story even made it into the papers, one of them asking their readers to send in other examples of 'ridiculous desk policies'. The company withdrew its regulations regarding the number of personal items allowed at each desk.

(Barnes, 2007)

65
The View in Tasmania and the Influence in Queensland

When the big Queensland office was about to renovate its inner-city site, the employees were given some influence over the design of the workplace. Their suggestions were accepted and put into practice; for example, airflow at the desks, tiles that reduced noise, good-quality chairs, levers to move keyboards up and down, and showers. The employees were very satisfied with their physical work environment.

When the company built a new site in Tasmania, it was modelled on the Queensland site because it had been such a success. The company did not think, however, that it was necessary to involve the workers this time. The whole site was designed without any worker influence at all. The office was very picturesquely located in a garden by a river, but only senior managers could see the view. The office only had small windows and the blinds were constantly drawn because the workers could not operate them – only top managers could open and shut their blinds. One worker commented: 'There is an outside world out there and people want to see it. . . . Why even have windows? Why do that to people? It feels like we're trapped.'

The workers accepted the reason for the blinds, which was to reduce eye-strain and headaches, but they had better solutions. Tinted windows, they said, would have had the same effect, still allowing them to look at the beautiful scenery every now and then. Management had not asked the employees and they had not thought of this themselves, which is why they were quite surprised that this replica of the appreciated site in an inner city location in Queensland met with such dissatisfaction beside a river in a park in Tasmania.

(Barnes, 2007)

66
Keeping up the Conversation

The line foreman called a meeting with all the gellers and said: 'From now on there will be no radio playing or talking when gelling. If you talk, you will be issued a warning. Three warnings and you're out of here.' Soon, long letters, written on paper napkins, started to circulate among the workers in order to keep up their conversations. That was one way of maintaining human dignity when faced with the ban on communicating with their fellow workers.

(Devinatz, 2007)

67
The Flight Attendant Who Did Not Smile

Flight attendants must always smile. Not an artificial smile, but a genuine one – it must be visible that it comes from within. At the same time, the airlines have constantly been increasing the number of passengers whom flight attendants have to take care of and smile at. Their answer has been to smile less, and when they do smile, it is not always in a genuine way. This resistance gets extra nourishment from a story about a heroine. It goes as follows. A businessman complained to a flight attendant that she did not smile at him. She put down her tray, looked him straight in the eye and said: 'I'll tell you what. You smile first, then I'll smile.' The businessman agreed and smiled. 'Good', she said. 'Now freeze, and hold that for fifteen hours.' And then she picked up her tray and left.

(Hochschild, 2003)

68
The Smile Strike

The hotel manager wanted to engage 'shoppers', but she met with opposition from the desk clerks. Shoppers are secretly employed by management to pose as customers, clients, passengers, policyholders and so on. Their task is to pass on information to management about the quality of service given by the employees. Generally, service employees regard this as spying and an unfair, dignity-threatening type of quality control. So did the hotel clerks.

When they found out about the hotel manager's plans, they became so angry that they staged a specific form of strike: they refused to smile at the customers. The hotel guests were treated correctly and speedily, but without feeling. They did not get one single smile.

(Fuller and Smith, 1991)

69
Writing Resistance

At my faculty at the university, all teachers and researchers are summoned to attend an administrative meeting. If I am unable to attend, I have to notify a manager because the meeting is obligatory, but I cannot be bothered. I do not have time for administrative meetings. I am doing my real work – I am writing a book of narratives about resistance.

Part III
Concepts

Although employee misbehaviour may not always lead to significant change, it is likely to remain a crucially important feature of workplace life, one that will continue to require detailed examination by critical scholars of work and organizations.

(Collinson and Ackroyd, 2005: 322)

70
Organizational Misbehaviour

In the narratives, we have met people in many occupations, in a good deal of industries, and in different countries. Nobody knows quite how widespread resistance and organizational misbehaviour are in working life, although there are estimates saying that 85 per cent or more of employees 'routinely behave in a manner that can be described as either deliberately deviant or intentionally dysfunctional' (Harris and Ogbonna, 2006: 543). There are also a variety of forms – ranging from feelings of cynicism to sabotaging machines, and from a surreptitious cup of coffee to a wildcat strike. Even if we do not have the exact numbers, we can assume that, in all probability, some form of organizational misbehaviour and resistance is present in all workplaces (cf. Ackroyd and Thompson, 1999: Ch. 7).

If we want to be able to understand and analyse all of this, we will need to use concepts as tools for thought. In the narratives, as well as in Chapter 1, I was slightly vague about the terminology. The reason for this was that I wanted to let the narratives speak for themselves without the reader having to worry about how to analyse them. In this part of the book, however, I will suggest an approach to rule-breaking and a model for analysing organizational misbehaviour in a partly novel way. In this chapter, I discuss the central point of misbehaviour: that is, breaking superiors' rules. I argue that this requires a different set, or sets, of rules, which employees can draw on when breaking their superiors' rules. The argumentation is based on empirical case studies of health care workers whose social position in their workplaces provides them with alternative sets of rules on which to base their actions with regard to their clients.

In the next and final chapter, I take my point of departure in the fact that there is a great variety of concepts in the literature in the field, expressing different perspectives that partly overlap and partly constitute different distinctions. I discuss a number of approaches and relate them to each other, hoping to reinforce the analysis within this research area. The concepts are organizational misbehaviour, resistance, abusive supervision, employee collective discipline and private business.

I regard organizational misbehaviour as the generic term for the field in question. Ackroyd and Thompson (1999: 2) defined organizational misbehaviour as 'anything you do at work you are not supposed to do'. As this is set in the workplace, we can note an important aspect of organizational misbehaviour: it is the superiors who decide, through their position in the power hierarchy of the work organization, what will count as misbehaviour and what will not. Later, they added that these things have to be done deliberately, formulating it as 'self-conscious rule-breaking' (Collinson and Ackroyd, 2005: 306). With an ironic twist, Ackroyd and Thompson (1999) use the term 'misbehaviour' in opposition to the tradition of Organizational Behaviour, where it is taken for granted that employees always do what management wants them to do: that is, they always follow the rules. A matter complicating the Organizational Behaviour approach, as well as the organizational misbehaviour approach, is that a well-known form of resistance lies in precisely following all the rules, that is 'working to rule', something that has made jurists raise the issue of whether or not working to rule really does breach an employment contract (Napier, 1972). When employees follow all the rules, the work process quickly breaks down. A worker at a newspaper printing office explains: 'If you followed all the safety regulations, I don't think the paper would ever be published on time. *But it's understood that you do things that you're not allowed to do in order for things to flow.*' (Wiklund, 2007: 73; my emphasis and translation). Here is a description of what happens when working to rule:

> Employees do exactly what is required by the regulations developed by the railway authorities. The result is that hardly any train leaves on time, schedules go haywire, and the whole railway system quickly slows to a snail's pace if not to a halt. The rules of course were created to control employees, to protect the safety of

passengers, and, equally important, to protect the railway authorities, since in the event of a major accident a clear structure of rules and responsibilities can help allocate blame. The only trouble is that there are so many rules that they render the railway system almost inoperable. *Normal functioning thus requires that employees find shortcuts or at least streamline procedures.* (Morgan, 1986: 164–5; my emphasis; cf. Gurley Flynn, 1997: 16–18 [1916])

In other words, organizational behaviour (following all the rules) is organizational misbehaviour (breaking them), and a certain amount of organizational misbehaviour is necessary if work is to be done. Employees are not supposed, in practice, to do exactly as they are formally supposed to do; they are also supposed to use their own judgement and creativity to make work happen – a phenomenon sometimes called 'necessary deviance' (Hoffman, 2008) or 'cooperative transgression' (Linhart, 1982). It can even be the case that managers explicitly try to persuade employees to break the rules, as in this case from a library when a manager talks about her problems with a supervisor:

I tried explaining to (the employee) a number of times that as a supervisor, *it was his responsibility to break the rules, to bend the rules*, to do what the patron needed to have done. He didn't get it and it made him angry. He would argue with me very gently, but he would argue with me. He'd say this is the way it's done throughout the library system and now you're telling me you don't do it the same way it's done elsewhere. And I'd say, that's right. He didn't understand what I was asking of him. He would fall back on the rules. (Balser and Stern, 1999: 1041; my emphasis)

Not just any action that breaks management rules can per se be regarded as organizational misbehaviour. The social work situation, defined by the social relations involved in each case, is the decisive criterion. Ackroyd and Thompson (1999: 81) treat this question as one of four factors – 'the extent to which the behaviour is functional to efficiency, profitability or "good order"' – that 'affect the judgements managers make about the appropriateness and likely effectiveness of taking action against specific instances of potential misbehaviour'. I think it is more than that: working to rule is a basic paradox of organizational misbehaviour. It follows, for example, that notions of workplaces in which there is no room for resistance must be met with scepticism. Because of the production indeterminacy of labour, some organizational misbehaviour, some conscious rule-breaking on the part of employees, must exist. Most importantly, however, it follows that organizational misbehaviour is not a specific set of actions, but actions that break rules that are in place in each specific situation within the power hierarchy at the workplace. What these actions are can vary – an action is sometimes organizational misbehaviour, sometimes not.

This emphasis on social relations leads to the need to supplement the definition of organizational misbehaviour. I would like to include two other dimensions in the concept of organizational misbehaviour: 'anything you are, do and think at work which you are not supposed to be, do and think'. In relation to the original definition, the verbs 'are' and 'think' have been added; they mark identity. Even if it is what people do, that it is their actions, that count in the final analysis, there are three further reasons why I think these processes should be included in the definition. The first concerns the enormous resources that employers put into indoctrinating their employees' thinking and identities via corporate culture. Although this is a very difficult endeavour, it is extremely attractive for employers to try to establish 'a culture devised by management and transmitted, marketed, sold or imposed on the rest of the organization' (Linstead and Grafton-Small, 1992: 333). The degree of success of this can be called into doubt, but it is clear that many employers think it is worth a try on a rather grand scale. The second reason concerns the reactions of workers to management's attempts to impose company culture on them, such as the ones we have encountered in some of the narratives: Management tries 'to get inside your head' (Ezzamel, Willmot and Worthington, 2004: 289); 'Basically, they are trying to change your personality' (McKinlay and Taylor, 1998: 179); and 'they were trying to brainwash me' (Huzell, 2009: 179). These cultural clashes, if I may call them that, should be reflected in the concept of misbehaviour. Other identities – for example, man or woman; member of a counterculture, a worker's collectivity or an occupational culture; consumer, football player or literature enthusiast – appear as rivals. Employees who do not embrace the culture of the company are misbehaving. Finally, Ackroyd and Thompson themselves emphasize that identity is important for organizational misbehaviour. They say, for example, that 'without the formation of a distinct identity by employees, any and all other forms of misbehaviour are difficult to envisage' (1999: 26). Bringing it all together, I propose the following definition of organizational misbehaviour: 'anything you consciously are, do and think at work that you are not supposed to be, do and think'.

Almost everything that occurs in the narratives can be classified as organizational misbehaviour: the nap on the mattress behind the staircase, the exotic dancers' choice of music, the plant managers' way of organizing work according to other principles than the ones prescribed by senior company managers, the cocktail waitresses' manoeuvrings in order to increase their tips, the recalcitrant factory workers' efforts to evade planned flexibility and so on. There is, however, one narrative that, at first sight, does not seem to qualify as misbehaviour, namely the one about the managers who deprived the toy factory workers of the possibility of adjusting the speed of the production line (Chapter 17). This does not concern, in any self-evident sense, organizational misbehaviour since no one in a superior position wanted something else. The managers' interference impacted on the autonomy of their subordinates; they simply used their position of power to declare this employee influence on work to be organizational misbehaviour.

Incidentally, I want to call the toy factory managers' actions 'blocking': they wanted to block the workers' influence on their work. More generally, we can regard blocking as management's riposte against the employees' organizational misbehaviour. However, if we go even higher up in the hierarchy, we find that the blocking carried out by these toy factory managers was, in fact, organizational misbehaviour. Senior management's position in the hierarchy was as agents of capital – their task was to make sure that the shareholders received as great a return as possible on their investment. When managers lower down in the hierarchy put their own control over the labour process above productivity and profit, they were misbehaving in relation to the owners (cf. Ackroyd and Thompson, 1999: 86).

My contention is that organizational misbehaviour, out of all the concepts being used within the research field, is the widest one because every narrative example falls under it. This is because any act, thought or identity can constitute misbehaviour, depending on the relations in existence at any one given time between superiors and subordinates within the hierarchy of the workplace. The same cannot be said about 'resistance', 'dissent', 'sabotage' and so on, which all have narrower meanings. This is the topic of the next chapter. To make my reasoning there clear, I first need to go into what organizational misbehaviour's central aspect of breaking rules entails.

Rationales of breaking management rules – An empirical example

With Jörg W. Kirchhoff[1]

In order to consciously break one rule, you follow another – there is no such thing as rule-free rule-breaking. Deliberately breaking a rule involves the rule-breaker drawing on a rule that he or she thinks overrides the first one. 'The (intentional) act of rebelling,' Tony Lawson (2003: 37) points out, 'requires as much knowledge of the rules as does that of conforming.' In this section, we describe mechanisms that legitimize organizational misbehaviour, that is rules providing the rationales for breaking management rules. The identification and analysis of work relations between the agents in an organization, as well as the rules developed within these relations, provide us with, we suggest, a better understanding of organizational behaviour and misbehaviour in the workplace. We discuss this against the backdrop of an empirical study of occupational groups in the Norwegian health service.

Questions regarding the nature of rules form part of the long and intense debate taking place in the social sciences on whether or not social structures exist, and, if they do, what they consist of. We will not, however, be entering into this debate here; let us simply declare that we side with critical realism positions and obtain assistance from the underlabouring of this philosophy. Our perspective on rules is as follows. Rules are connected to positions (or 'slots') in social structures. A social structure is constructed by internally related positions, such as employer–employee or home care assistant–client, meaning that one side of the relationship cannot exist without the other. There are interrelated networks or 'latticeworks' of relations (Fleetwood, 2008: 258–259) attached to positions, each connected to certain rules. Rules, like institutions and social structures, emerge from human actions. However, rules differ ontologically from human actions. As rules have emergent powers – they are the result of human actions, but they have powers that cannot be reduced to these actions or the individuals who perform them – they are to some extent autonomous from the social group that made them. Therefore, social rules and human agency cannot be reduced to each other. Consequently, in an analytical perspective, rules always exist prior to the actions that relate to them. Nonetheless, rules cannot predict actions – there is an ontological gap between them.

Rules are injunctions and they take the form 'if x do y under conditions z' (Lawson, 2003: 36). Of course, 'x' is something to be achieved – rules are directed toward goals – while 'y' is an action that the rule prescribes in order to achieve the goal. Thus far, this is quite a common definition of a rule. For example, Bunge (1998: 332) provides this formulation: 'To attain goal G, perform action A.' But in Lawson's critical realist conception, the action always takes place in a specific space-time and sociocultural context, 'z'. An example of a management rule in the work of a home care assistant could be: 'To do your work properly (x), clean the floor and do the dishes (y) when visiting client NN's house (z).'

Even though rules in working life are most obviously connected to bureaucratic organizations, they exist in all organizations. In fact, it is impossible to imagine an organization without rules. At the same time, rules cannot be expected to be followed in any strict sense; in workplaces, they are constantly treated as objects of interpretation, experimentation and struggle, and they are always being 'interpreted in action' (Edwards, 1986: 81). Further, there are different sets of rules in workplaces, connected to different structural positions. These positions are part of what we generally term 'work forms,' defined as internal social relations in working life (Karlsson, 2004). Our concern here is wage labour, which initially consists of the relation between employer and employee. In exploring the rules in workplaces, our starting point, therefore, is management rules. These are the rules that employees are supposed to follow but that they break while committing organizational misbehaviour. What we are searching for are the rules on which they draw when misbehaving. This question revolves around agents' interactions in relation to different sets of rules connected to different work relations. In our study of different occupational groups in the health care sector, we have, more concretely, found service rules in relation to the client, employee collective rules within workgroups and professional employee rules in relation to a profession based outside the workplace – all related to each other and to the clients.

The study: Design and methods

The data presented are derived from organizational case studies of employees in four local health care enterprises within two municipalities in Norway (Kirchhoff, 2010). These enterprises were selected on the basis that they were organised in accordance with the purchaser–provider model, inspired by New Public Management (NPM) reforms aimed at improving efficiency in public organizations, which will soon be presented in detail. The employees of these organizations consisted of four occupational groups: registered nurses; auxiliary nurses and care workers, providing primary health care services; and home care assistants providing domestic services. In order to cover all the services provided by these enterprises, the study sample was constructed by selecting employees from within all of the occupational groups in each enterprise.

In order to understand the context and content of employees' work, participant observation at the beginning of the study was utilised to observe them at work. His background as a registered nurse gave Jörg Kirchhoff the opportunity to work with one informant from each occupation in all four organizations for one day, and thus to gather information about the services being provided and the employees' interactions with their clients and the other employees. This information was summed up in field notes and analysed in order to construct a semistructured interview guide ahead of the next phase of data compilation, which consisted of focus group and individual in-depth interviews. Even though the interviews were based on a semistructured interview guide, new issues and topics were added when these were considered to be of relevance to the study. At the end of the study, the main content of an interview consisted of the following issues: the overall content of employee services provided to clients; employee attitudes to management rules; their relationships with clients, colleagues and other members of the organization; and the ways in which employees legitimize services that deviate from management rules.

Focus group interviews were the primary interview method, but difficulties in establishing the focus groups meant that 4 of the 16 interviews became individual in-depth interviews. However, employees from each occupation in each organization were represented and they provided information about their work, their attitudes to management rules and their rationale when breaking them. Employees were selected if they worked for at least 75 per cent of a full-time position. All the interviews were based on informed consent, digitally recorded and depersonalized during transcription.

The local health care enterprises

In Norway, health and social services are public services, based on and regulated via legislation, and administered by municipal authorities. Since 1990, they have undergone comprehensive reforms, inspired by concepts related to NPM (Rasmussen, 2004; Vabø, 2005). NPM is portrayed as a response to budget crises, failures in economic policy and a rigid bureaucratic public administration, becoming in the early 1980s the answer to expansive, expensive and inflexible public sectors in the United States and Europe (Rasmussen, 2004; Simonet, 2008). NPM consists of several central principles, for example, the use of market forces to serve public purposes, the principle of individual manager accountability, the need for competition within the public sector through the use of contracts, close attention to the outcome of public sector activities and concern for standards that regulate the public sector (Hannigan, 1998; Simonet, 2008; Vabø, 2005; Wilkinson, 1995). In sum, these principles emphasize the importance of changing public sector organizations into business companies and they represent a shift from public administration to public management.

The purchaser–provider model encompasses many of these principles and was imported from the United States to the United Kingdom in the early 1990s (Hannigan, 1998); it was introduced to Scandinavia during the 1990s (Green-Pedersen, 2002; Rasmussen, 2004; Vabø, 2005). According to this model, municipalities are reorganized into two separate organizational units: the administration of health and social services becomes the purchaser organization, and the institutions providing health and social services become the provider organization. Through this split, the municipality can invite tenders in order to find the most cost-efficient provider. In 2004, almost 30 per cent of all Norwegian municipalities were organising their health and social services in accordance with the purchaser–provider model; this involved almost 50 per cent of the Norwegian population, since it was mostly large municipalities that had introduced the model (Ramsdal and Hansen, 2005).

Inspired by NPM, all the enterprises in our study were organized in accordance with the purchaser–provider model. In practice, this model leads to an employee of a purchaser enterprise deciding whether or not clients who request public services are entitled to them, and then ordering a provider enterprise to provide the services. These instructions were stated in service contracts that defined in detail the type, regularity and content of services to clients. Consequently, service contracts became a management rule for determining the standard of services delivered by employees in provider enterprises, resulting in robust restrictions on employees' possibilities of controlling their work.

All the enterprises had a similar formal organizational structure, despite some minor differences. They employed staff from comparable occupational categories, provided both health and social services, and were organized using the same structure, that of an administrative manager at the top and a large staff of employees at the bottom of the hierarchy. Although the formal structure of the enterprises appeared simple on an organizational map, differences between employees regarding the distribution of formal academic education resulted in a differentiated social structure of positions and differences in the distribution of the tasks provided by each occupational group. First, due to their professional status, registered nurses were placed in administrative positions, where they managed enterprises and were authorized to manage medical issues. Registered nurses thus provided clients with advanced medical services, in addition to basic health care services, and they supervised other employees in other occupations in their work. Second, auxiliary nurses and care workers, possessing basic medical knowledge, were certified to provide basic health services, that is, to take care of clients' essential medical needs. Finally, home care assistants were employees without any formal education, and thus not certified to provide health services; these employees were assigned solely to domestic services, for example, vacuuming clients' apartments or cleaning windows.

A formal education thus contributed to a social structure among the occupations, with registered nurses at the top and home care assistants at the bottom of the work organization hierarchy. As a consequence, the rationales for breaking management rules differed between employees, since their social position within the enterprise resulted in variations in work relations with different rationales.

Findings

The overall content of the health and social services provided to clients can be categorized into two types: services in accordance with management rules and services neither defined nor regulated by management rules. The latter type mostly consisted of additional services, provided by employees from all occupational categories in all enterprises. These services were neither expected nor wanted by management and were usually in conflict with management rules, that is, the service contracts standardizing the services provided to clients. Therefore, additional services provided to clients can be categorized as organizational misbehaviour. The phenomenon of employees breaking organizational rules in order to satisfy clients, patients or customers has been noted before, especially in the management literature; it has, for example, been conceptualized as 'pro-social rule breaking' (Morrison, 2006) or 'responsible subversion' (Hutchinson, 1990). These analyses do not, however, ask which rules this rule-breaking is based on.

The rationales for providing these additional services, and in doing so breaching the service contract, differed between employees and were related to three distinct categories of rules, namely, service rules, collective rules and professional rules. Furthermore, these rules were based on three distinctive categories of work relations between the agents of the enterprises, that is, client–employee work relations, collegial work relations and work relations among the professionals in the enterprises. In order to understand the emergence of 'rule-breaking', the content of management rules must be presented.

The content and influence of management rules

The management rules consisted of legal and organizational rules. The legal rules found expression in laws and judicial instructions and were related to legal conditions for public services, job qualification requirements and interactions between employees and clients, which established legal working conditions and thus avoided judicial review by the authorities. In addition, the management rules also consisted of organizational rules for interpreting the legal rules in an organizational context: these were rules to place employees in a social position in the organization; rules to define the interrelationships of these positions; and rules regarding how to organize, coordinate and distribute work.

Although management rules varied between organizations, mainly because of different organizational rules, their influence on the employees was the same. First, management rules emphasized medical knowledge as being crucial to the work, thereby establishing a hierarchical structure of social positions within the enterprise, with registered nurses at the top and home care assistants at the bottom of the pyramid. In addition, medical knowledge had an impact on the distribution of work and on employee autonomy, resulting in greater autonomy among registered nurses than among employees in other occupations. Second, management rules, in the form of service contracts, defined the content and number of the employees' services to their clients by means of standards and instructions regarding the work and the processes involved. The service contract was a legal document that was based on citizens' civil rights regarding public services and specified the content and number of services to be provided to individual clients. In doing so, the service contract became a legal standardization of the employees' work. For example: 'Vacuum clean the apartment once a week and clean the windows twice a year' would be a normal service contract relating to social services, whereas 'Dress the wound on the left leg and administer the client's medication' serves as an example of a contract relating to health services.

Despite the differences between the contents of service contracts relating to health or social services, these contracts restricted the employees to providing no further services than those defined within them. Therefore, management was constantly emphasising that the service contract was the main management rule for the employees:

> I always say to them, the service contract tells you what to do. If you deliver your car to the garage for a service control, they

have a procedure to follow, and that is what you are paying for. It's what you expect them to do. You can't polish the car, or change its colour, or do more – whatever they are. The organization would suffer from a deficit. We wouldn't make it financially. (Manager)

This quotation illustrates management's instrumental view of the service contract. Based on a financial argument, its purpose was to ring-fence the employees' duties, to confine their work. The resources of the organizations were regulated by service contracts, and additional services provided to clients would result in organizational imbalances. The employees recognized this, although they sometimes found it hard to provide services confined to the contract.

Interviewer: Do you have any kind of work instruction to follow?
Care worker 1: Yes, we have service contracts we must comply with.
Interviewer: And there it tells you in detail what to do?
Care worker 2: Yes. On the whole we do what they say, but not
                 always.

Although employees generally acknowledged the importance of management rules and referred to them as 'guidelines for work', the above quotation serves to show that the employees did not always comply with their service contracts. Independently of their occupational or organizational background, the employees often consciously violated this management rule (the service contract). On these occasions, they provided services outside the service contract by providing alternative or additional services, which were neither expected nor wanted by management.

The employees' main reason for doing so was to meet their clients' needs, as presented by the clients to the employees during the delivery of social or health services. The employees then had to decide whether to reject the clients' requests or accede to them, breaking management rules in doing so. Therefore, the point of departure when breaking management rules was an acknowledgment of the clients' needs. However, even though the clients' needs gave rise to the issue of rule-breaking, the rationales for breaking management rules differed between employees and were related to different categories of rules at the companies. We start our discussion of this by using the category of service rules.

The rationale for service rules

Service rules are informal rules or tacit agreements that evolve through an interpersonal relationship between employees and their clients, that is, through an informal client–employee work relationship. This relationship is based on, and related to, the formal employer–employee relationship, since this relationship also constitutes the employee's relationship with the client, that is, by the provision of services based on management rules. Following these rules, the employees became acquainted with their clients and simultaneously developed an informal work relationship within the formal work relationship, and then service rules took form. Therefore, all employees across all occupations established an informal client–employee work relationship. However, this work relationship was strongest among the home care assistants and provided their main rationale for breaking management rules. In earlier studies, it has been noted that the relationship between the home care worker and her client can become so intimate that she becomes 'fictive kin' (Karner, 1998). Further, Aronson and Neysmith (1996: 66) found that these workers 'commonly used the language of friendships and family relations to describe their ties with clients'.

The constitution and strength of the service rules used by home care assistants were related to three different structural aspects of their work. First, employees within this occupation had a fragile employer–employee connection as a result of their position of social isolation within the organization. They were seldom in contact with the other employees or with management, since they worked alone in the homes of their clients and rarely reported on or discussed their work with other colleagues or management. Furthermore, the other employees rarely gave them a hand when help was needed, or listened to their problems at meetings. Therefore, the clients were their primary contacts at work, and their relationships with their clients became vital:

> I'm only at the office half an hour a day. Most of the time I'm together with my clients. They are my workplace, not the office. Having a good relationship with my clients out there is much more important to me than with employees in here [the office]. (Home care assistant)

Second, the inherent structure of their work led to long-lasting encounters with clients and provided good conditions for the development of a strong informal client–employee work relationship. To begin with, home care assistants provided their clients with social services over a long period of time, often until clients died and new ones were added to their list. In addition, the nature of the social services provided resulted in prolonged interactions with clients: cleaning a flat could, for example, take up to an hour. Therefore, enduring encounters between clients and home care assistants, as a result of the structure of the assistants' work, provided an opportunity for the establishment of strong social bonds.

Third, no home care assistant enjoyed her work, since the tasks were monotonous, led to physical stress and were far from stimulating. These negative characteristics of the home care assistants' work made them value a good, close and informal relationship with their clients, since this relationship provided them with an opportunity to enhance the quality of their working conditions.

Interviewer:	How is work? Good, bad?
Home care assistant 1:	It's monotonous and sometimes boring.
Several voices:	That's true.
Home care assistant 1:	Every day is the same.
Home care assistant 2:	On the other hand you have all these nice clients. You meet other people. That's okay. But I'd gladly avoid doing housework if I could.
Home care assistant 3:	That's true. Housework is monotonous, but since it puts us in touch ... with all kinds of people it's easier to put up with.

In sum, the social position of the home care assistants at the company, the enduring encounters with clients and the negative characteristics of the work all enhanced the importance of an informal client–employee work relationship, thus weakening the formal employer–employee work relationship. Therefore, service rules provided alternative working rules with a rationale for breaking management rules, for example, providing additional services prohibited by management. While service rules tended to be connected to an individual relationship with a client, the next type of rule is collective.

The rationale for collective rules

Collective rules constitute a collective understanding and interpretation of work and work- related issues; they evolve in consequence of the formal and informal interactions between employees in the workplace. This interaction was based on a network of collegial work relations, as a result of the social position of the employees within the organization. It constituted and maintained collective rules through employees' working together, participating in discussions about procedures and sharing experienced encounters with clients and others in the workplace.

Collegial work relations existed in all of the companies and provided the basis for collective rules. However, collegial work relations were in place only among the employees providing health services, that is, registered nurses, auxiliary nurses and care workers, since these were organized into teams. Each team shared a pool of clients, and the team members were thus in frequent contact in order to distribute and coordinate work and to share information about clients. Additionally, all the teams in a company interacted on a daily basis, for example, at lunch breaks and at report meetings where employees exchanged information about work-related issues. Therefore, the social position of the employees as team members placed them in collegial work relations, which provided a foundation for collective rules on how to interpret management rules, how to perform and distribute work, and the extent to which the employees should meet their clients' needs and thus break management rules.

Working as team members resulted in collective interpretations of management rules, since there was a common understanding that these rules, that is, the service contract, had to be adjusted to make sense of the team members' work. Thus, the employees redefined their job through collective discussions.

Interviewer:	About this service contract, when you visit clients, does the contract match their needs?
Care worker 1:	Not always.
Care worker 2:	Then we change them. Contracts can be reformulated.

Interviewer:	Who changes the content of the service contract, can anyone do that?
Care worker 1:	Well, we discuss it when we're giving the report at the end of the day.
Care worker 2:	That is right, when we report. No changes can be made until we've discussed it. You can't just go there and change it.
Care worker 1:	No, you can't do that on your own.
Care worker 2:	It must be discussed before you make any changes.

Collective discussions could lead to adjustments being made to the service contract when management rules were regarded as not being fully relevant to a client's needs. However, adjustment did not necessarily conflict with management rules, since discussions often led to a better understanding of them. Sometimes, however, collective discussions and collective rules provided a basis for overriding management rules, for example, by providing services in accordance with clients' needs, even though these needs were not defined in the contract.

Interviewer:	To what extent do service contracts regulate your work?
Auxiliary nurse 1:	Not at all, they don't regulate what I do in any detail.
Several voices:	No, not at all.
Auxiliary nurse 2:	A service contract might restrict the services we offer to dressing a wound, for example, but the client has to have something to eat as well. Or we do the dishes. We have to adjust our services to the client's needs.

Although management's interpretation of service contracts resulted in restrictions being placed on health services, the above quotation illustrates the collective understanding on the part of the employees that all the needs of the client had to be taken into account when health services were being provided.

There were also, however, disagreements among employees as to the extent to which they should meet their clients' needs. These disagreements mainly concerned service rules, based as they were on a great variety of individual, informal client–employee work relations. This frequently resulted in discussions and arguments about where to 'draw the line' as regards the clients' needs. Employees at all the companies had disagreements about this and even categorized their colleagues as 'good' or 'bad' employees, where good employees made more extensive efforts to meet their clients' requests than did bad employees. Consequently, tensions emerged between good and bad employees, becoming a potential source of conflict at the company. Collective rules, through providing collective compliance with individual requests from clients, offered a means of coping with these disagreements and thus of avoiding conflicts. This is illustrated by a conflict between good and bad colleagues about picking up a client's newspaper, which led to informal negotiations resulting in an agreement. One nurse said:

Nurse: Well, I'll have to give and take a bit. And then everybody has to agree that we're going to do it that way. Then the client has to bring in the newspaper herself, even though I'd like to be able to do her that favour. Because we all jointly agreed that she has to do it herself, and that everybody has to act in accordance with our agreement.

The statement illustrates how negotiations between employees generate and reinforce collective norms, thus affecting additional services. In consequence, collective rules restrain the number of services provided by the good employees and become a mechanism of collective control.

Collective rules, then, were related to health services in different ways as they interpreted management rules, restricted informal service rules, and provided a rationale for breaking management rules. Although collective rules influenced the employees and their work at all the companies, the impact of these rules varied between the organizations. One reason for this was differences in the number of professional employees, that is, registered nurses, between the organizations, and the strength of professional rules among registered nurses, our last rationale for breaking management rules. This, too, is collective, but it is based on a collective stretching across the organizations: the profession of registered nurse.

The rationale for professional rules

Contrary to management, service and collective rules, professional rules are established outside the organization and are the result of formal academic education, providing their own standards in relation to health services. These rules are sustained and reinforced by the professionals working in organizations in order to legitimize professional working standards, which often override management rules when the rules are in conflict with professional standards. The only occupational group that referred to professional knowledge in their arguments regarding the necessity of overruling the service contract was registered nurses. Studies of nurses' resistance have mostly concerned their relationship with doctors (Bolton, 2004), less frequently their relationship with management (Timmons, 2003); however, it is the latter relationship we will deal with here.

Registered nurses maintained and reinforced professional rules through formal and informal interactions with other professionals, and in doing so realized a professional community that consisted of work relations between professionals. In order to establish and strengthen their professional work relations, registered nurses made efforts to meet regularly for professional discussions, sometimes even in their spare time, during which they talked about and reflected on their work and relationships with clients and colleagues. Thus, the work relations of professionals maintained their professional rules.

Furthermore, the organizational structure provided good conditions for the professionals and their standards, often resulting in the transformation of professional rules into management rules. First, the organization's acknowledgment of professional knowledge resulted in the registered nurses' control over their work processes, since their education qualified them to perform medical services without supervision. Registered nurses were frequently also responsible for the preparation of procedures for specific health services, for example, a protocol regarding how to dress a client's wound. In consequence, this protocol became a management rule that was based on the registered nurses' professional standards. Second, having a formal education gave the registered nurses the authority to supervise and instruct employees lacking formal academic training for their service work.

Interviewer:	What do you mean when you refer to nurses' responsibility? How does it make a difference to other employees of this organization?
Registered nurse 1:	We guide our other colleagues at work.
Interviewer:	Do you do that a lot?

Registered nurse 1:	Well, it happens. They [auxiliary nurses and care workers] come to us and ask for our help and advice in various situations.
Registered nurse 2:	We have some kind of supervisory responsibility for them.
Interviewer:	What do you mean by supervisory responsibility?
Registered nurse 2:	We have to ensure that they do their job properly. In a justifiable way, you know.
Registered nurse 3:	After all, we have more professional knowledge than they do. So it's only natural.

The nurses' professional knowledge confirmed their social position within the organization and led to an acceptance of their supervision of the other employees. Although the professional rules were frequently complied with, and influenced management rules, they could also come into conflict with the service contract when it interfered with professional work processes.

For the registered nurses, professional work entailed several processes, mainly making diagnoses, administering medical treatment and evaluating the health services provided to clients. Furthermore, each process was related to their body of professional knowledge.

You have to use your head. That's what we learnt at nursing school. You have to consider all needs since they are interrelated, for example, physical and mental conditions. (Registered nurse)

In contrast to this professional approach, service contracts could enforce other standards than their own on the registered nurses, since a purchaser was diagnosing and making decisions about the treatment of a client. Furthermore, the registered nurses often perceived their professional diagnosis to be diverging from the diagnosis and treatment specified in service contracts. Therefore, they rejected service contracts when these contracts were in conflict with their own professional standards. When asked about the impact of the service contract on their work, some registered nurses answered as follows:

Interviewer:	Did service contracts from the purchaser change your job?
Registered nurse 2:	No, I don't think so.
Registered nurse 1:	You see, most of the contracts didn't match the reality. So you couldn't work in the way contracts ordered you to.
Registered nurse 3:	Because, if you worked in accordance with the contract, the client wouldn't receive the correct health service. The contract was like a map that didn't match the terrain.

The nurses' misbehaviour in relation to the service contracts was based on their professional rule of diagnosing clients in accordance with their professional knowledge. Hence, this professional knowledge provided the basis for rules with a rationale for breaking management rules.

In addition to rules based on their professional knowledge, the registered nurses also referred to ethical rules, that is, rules in accordance with their professional code, when breaking management rules. One of these rules was the holistic approach to clients, which implied an ambitious standard of care, thus providing a justification, and thus also an obligation, to meet all the needs of a client.

Interviewer:	This might be a bit provocative, but when you are short of time, that could be a result of doing more than you're required to in the contract?
Registered nurse 1:	What I do at work depends on the clients' need. You can't just go in and do your stuff; you've got to be human as well.
Registered nurse 2:	At nursing college, we learnt that there's a connection between mental issues and physical illness. Sure, I can do my job faster, just running in and out, giving them their medication, and writing my reports and so on. But that would result in depressed clients – you see, everything's connected.
Registered nurse 1:	Sure, I'd be better off just doing what I'm supposed to do. But I have to view my client holistically.

Being 'human' illustrated a caring rule implying that the registered nurses were obliged to meet their clients' needs, although these needs were without limit, since their holistic approach neither restricted nor ranked them. Therefore, ethical rules made it compulsory for the registered nurses to provide additional services when needed, and in doing so to deviate from the limitations of the service contracts.

In sum, professional knowledge and ethical rules were interrelated and constituted a set of professional rules providing a rationale for breaking management rules. Although professional rules were related to socialization during education, they were maintained through work relations between professionals, that is, the registered nurses. Therefore, the impact of professional rules on work was related to the strength of these work relations, even if the content of the professional rules was similar between companies.

Concluding discussion

The findings concerning additional services provided by the employees of health care companies are consistent with those of previous studies (Hutchinson, 1990; Morrison, 2006; Vabø, 2007). Næss (2003) concludes that almost all employees in the public health sector in Norway provide additional services at work, and, furthermore, 40 per cent of them offer help in their spare time. However, the mechanisms of doing this have not been adequately investigated. Therefore, our concluding discussion not only summarises the employees' rationales for breaking management rules but also elaborates on a theoretical framework in order to elucidate the emergence and conditions of rule-breaking.

Table 70.1 summarizes our findings by presenting three rationales, or distinctive rule sets, and thus answers our question regarding what rules employees invoke when they are breaking management rules. Furthermore, the table also provides an overview of how these rules were distributed between the employees across the various occupations working for public health care companies.

In addition to summarising our findings, Table 70.1 also illustrates the fact that there is an uneven distribution of rules between the occupations working in the various companies. Registered nurses could draw on all the rationales when they were deviating from the service contract. Auxiliary nurses and care workers could fall

Table 70.1 Rationales for breaking management rules at public health care companies

Occupation	Service rules	Collective rules	Professional rules
Registered nurse	√	√	√
Auxiliary nurse	√	√	
Care worker	√	√	
Home care assistant	√		

back on service rules and collective rules, while home care assistants gained their rationale for breaking management rules solely from service rules.

When there is more than one type of rule in the rule set for an occupation, there seems to be a tendency for one of them to become more important than the other(s). Service rules provided the rationale for home care assistants, mostly as a consequence of their isolated position within the organization, which resulted in a lack of other rules. For auxiliary nurses and care workers, collective rules provided the main rationale for breaking management rules, since these collective rules were shared by the majority of the employees. Collective rules defined the situations in which one could break management rules, as well as where to 'draw the line' regarding clients' needs. Thus, collective rules restricted the service rules between 'good' employees and clients. However, collective rules also made 'bad' employees extend their services to some degree. At one company, for example, the employees organized a shopping day for a client, although this kind of service went far beyond the organizational resources. In this case, collective rules were hierarchically ordered above service rules because of their potential to overrule both 'good' and 'bad' employees.

Finally, professional rules provided the dominant rationale for the registered nurses and were hierarchically ordered above collective rules, service rules and management rules; they were thus referred to most frequently when the nurses were breaking management rules. The acknowledgment by colleagues and management of professional rules was one cause of their superiority over other rule sets. The auxiliary nurses and care workers, for example, turned to the registered nurses in order to discuss clients and work-related issues, thus subordinating themselves to the standards of the registered nurses. In addition, the registered nurses were assigned by management to supervise work and work out procedures and other organizational rules, which reinforced their position and resulted in the acceptance of professional standards in the companies.

All in all, our findings show that organizational misbehaviour among employees can be related to different rules and rule sets, and that the various occupational groups referred to rule sets that were in part different when breaking management rules, although the outcome of rule-breaking in the form of provision of additional services was similar.

We relate the emergence of different rationales to distinctive work relations within the context of wage labour. The concept of work relation is based on rules, as mechanisms of action, being connected to positions within social structures, such as the position of the employee of a health care company. The social position of an employee in the context of wage labour is thus part of an employer–employee work relation, in which management rules are developed – at least in part – in order to control employees. In consequence, however, using this work relation and these management rules, employees were assigned to further social positions related to work. In our study, wage labour and management rules placed employees in relation to clients, colleagues and professionals in order to provide and coordinate services to clients. Therefore, as a result of an employer–employee work relation, other work relations that are dependent on the social structure of wage labour also emerge.

Figure 70.1 illustrates how wage labour leads to a social structure of work relations at health care companies, based on the employees' social positions in the organization.

The figure illustrates how, as a result of being employed, an employee can be placed in various, distinct work relations. The basic work relation in wage labour is the one between the employer and the employee, which leads to management rules for employees providing services to clients and rules about how to organize and coordinate work. In consequence, a number of other work relations emerge at the companies: between employees and clients, among employees in teams and among professionals. These relations form the basis of opposing sets of rules relative to management rules: service rules,

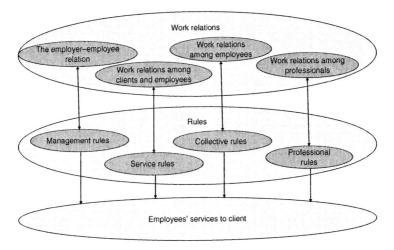

Figure 70.1 Work relations, rules and services at health care companies

collective rules and professional rules. As there is a gap between rules and activities, management rules will not automatically result in the provision of services to clients as laid down in the service contract. The actual services rendered are also affected by the other three rule sets, providing rationales for breaking management rules. Wage labour and management rules thus form the basis of contradictory outcomes: services both in accordance with service contracts and in the form of additional or alternative services – the latter breaking management rules.

We have tried to provide a further understanding of organizational misbehaviour, in which employees consciously break management rules, by presenting findings from case studies in four health care companies in Norway. Drawing on a critical realist perspective, we argue that wage labour results in a social structure that constitutes distinct sets of work relations; within these emerge different sets of rules, making up rationales for breaking management rules. Therefore, in order to comprehend employee behaviour and misbehaviour, we have to consider not only management rules but also work relations and rules in consequence of these relations. The findings of our study reveal three distinct rule sets, providing rationales for breaking management rules: service rules, collective rules and rules among professionals, based on different work relations between employees at the health care company. By satisfying what they defined as their clients' needs, they tried to maintain their dignity when the service contract and management rules restricted the services which they regarded as legitimate, on the basis of other rules, to provide their clients with what they needed. In order to perform dignified work, they had to misbehave.

*   *   *

Rules, then, are based on social relations and, in order to understand organizational misbehaviour, we need to take into account sets of rules other than those laid down by superiors. These are rules that help employees to keep their dignity. In the next chapter, I continue the discussion of organizational misbehaviour by relating this term to a number of other terms in the research field. I claim that it is fruitful to regard organizational misbehaviour as an overarching concept, and the other concepts as variants thereof.

71
Relations in the Workplace Power Hierarchy

In the literature on the concept of work, there is a contradiction between definitions that take their point of departure from a number of activities per se versus from any activity performed within specific social relations. In the first case, 'work activities tend to be seen as historical constants and as applicable to every member of a given society.' In the second case, 'an activity that is work during a given historical period, or in connection with a specific social category, can be non-work during another period or in connection with another social category' (Karlsson, 2004: 93). The same observations can be made concerning the literature on resistance. There is a contradiction between regarding resistance as a number of activities per se or as the activities that are performed within certain social relationships. In the first case, the activities are resistance whenever, wherever and within whatever social relations they occur. In the second case, an activity that is resistance in a specific social context can be something else in another; it all depends on the social relations involved. When one wishes to analyse resistance, one can, in the first case, immediately look for the specified activities; in the second case, one first has to find the specified social relations.

In this chapter I argue that the most fruitful way of approaching the field of organizational misbehaviour and resistance is to regard these phenomena from the perspective of social relations. The relations in question are those of the power hierarchy of superior and subordinate positions in workplaces. On the basis of these two theoretical principles, I build a conceptual model that, I suggest, can make a contribution to richer analyses of the field.

On the question of activities per se or activities in specific social relations, it is instructive to compare two articles on resistance by Randy Hodson (1991, 1995) in order to make the distinction more concrete. In the first article, he differentiates partly overlapping clusters of actions in the workplace. There are two dominating clusters of equal size, namely 'Enthusiastic Compliance' and 'Conditional Effort'. Then there are a number of smaller clusters, primarily arranged around conditional effort: 'Making Out', 'Foot-dragging', 'Withdrawal', 'Sabotage', 'Gossip and Infighting' and 'Brownnosing'. This is a model of workers' 'Behavioural Modes' in the workplace, constituting a typology of resistance. Its merit, Hodson says, is that it 'is based on an active view of the worker who is seen as constantly engaged in the social construction of the setting in which productive activity takes place' (1991: 73). He also offers some hypotheses about which social contexts the different actions are likely to occur in. There are two problems, I suggest, with this approach. One is that it tends to limit the analysis of resistance to a definite set of activities; it will obstruct possibilities of empirically finding types of resistance that are not included in the typology. The other is that these activities are always of resistance, independent of social context. In the stories, there are many examples of actions that would otherwise be thought of as resistance. However, in specific social circumstances, these are accepted by management and/or actually result in more efficient production. Remember the tale of the two aquatic centres (Chapter 11, based on Townsend, 2004). At one of them, the employees sat down and read or just took it easy when business was slow. In terms of Hodson's first article, this would be foot-dragging, but in this case, the owner encouraged the employees to relax when there were slack periods. One effect of this was that the employees worked hard without complaining when there were lots of customers. Another effect was that there was hardly any resistance at all in that workplace. A further example is the department that was so satisfied with the work done by Establishment Printers (Chapter 5, based on Button, Mason and Sharrock, 2003) – satisfaction that was due to the machine operators, administrators and first-line managers conspiring to maintain the workflow by breaking every rule there was. This included actions that, according to Hodson's first model, would be classified as sabotage. A final example is taking a nap. Remember the worker in Chapter 2 who had found a free space to sleep behind the stairs?

That was a clear case of 'withdrawal' in Hodson's terminology. But now there are research results that show that taking a nap at work enhances the productivity of workers, something that changes things entirely:

> By demonstrating the relationship between workplace napping and mental agility in both controlled studies and workplace settings, a new meaning of the nap is constructed. No longer simply a cloak-and-dagger act that cheats the company of productive labor, now the nap at work is a rational strategy for increasing productivity and extending the capacity for work.... Once a tactical, jerry-rigged private rebellion against the discipline of work, the workplace nap is an increasingly normalized activity that is integrated into the work role and the work day. Napping is tolerated or introduced at work to increase mental acuity and amplify efficiency in ever-demanding work environments. *It also normalizes a formerly covert practice into the rule-governed structure of organizations.* (Baxter and Kroll-Smith, 2005: 34, 50–1; my emphasis)

What used to be a classical rule-breaking practice has, in this American case, been turned into part of the organizational rules. In the Swedish workplace in Chapter 2, the nap is still forbidden, which makes apparent the deficiencies of basing the definition of resistance on activities per se.

In the second article, Hodson abandoned this Behavioural Modes approach in favour of a social relations approach. He now defines resistance as 'any individual or small-group act intended to mitigate claims by management on workers or to advance workers' claims against management' (1995: 80). Here, resistance is not regarded as specific actions per se but as elements of the relationship between management and workers in workplaces. Hodson goes on to relate management control strategies to forms of worker resistance. A direct personal control strategy is responded to by forms of resistance of deflecting abuse in order to maintain dignity. Against technical control, that is control by means of technical systems, the resistance strategy of regulating the amount and intensity of work is used. Defending autonomy by fighting over procedures for, and the organization of, tasks is the resistance strategy against bureaucratic control using formal rules and specified operational procedures. In relation to what he regards to be modern forms of control by means of worker influence via teams, the strategy is to develop and manipulate these possibilities. One should note that Hodson emphasizes that resistance strategies are not immediate reflections of control strategies; in concrete cases, both control and resistance are made up of mixtures of several strategies. All employee resistance strategies are, however, developed in relation to management control strategies, making it possible for this relational model to steer clear of the pitfalls of the activity model.

Let us now return to organizational misbehaviour, the topic of the former chapter. At the centre of organizational misbehaviour lies the hierarchy of command. Managers define which actions, thoughts and identities are organizational misbehaviour on the part of the workers while managers on high levels define what constitutes organizational misbehaviour on the part of managers on lower levels. This is a very broad conceptualization and the other terms I will discuss cover parts or subsets of misbehaviour. The conceptualization of organizational misbehaviour is relational, and it follows that these concepts – resistance, abusive supervision, employee collective discipline and private business – also have to be conceptually constructed as social relations rather than activities per se. Further, these concepts being subsets of organizational misbehaviour must also be taken into account when formulating the other terms. First, there should be the definition of organizational misbehaviour, which I presented in the previous chapter, but then there should also be another part that states what is specific to each term within this framework. As the power hierarchy is of key importance here, the latter part of the definitions has to be structured according to different directions in relation to this hierarchy within the workplace (Figure 71.1).

The pyramid symbolizes, of course, the command hierarchy in a workplace. Resistance is organizational misbehaviour that is directed upwards in the hierarchy towards managers or, in the case of managers, towards managers higher up. Abusive supervision goes in the opposite direction, consisting of managers harassing employees or senior managers harassing junior managers. In workers' own informal collective organizations – for example, in self-organizations or worker collectivities – there are cases where workers discipline other workers in order to put up a common front against management.

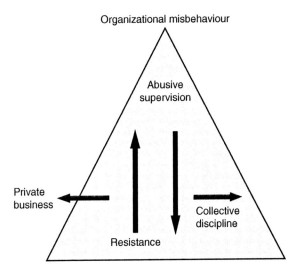

Figure 71.1 Subsets of organizational misbehaviour in relation to the command hierarchy

Finally, there are relations reaching out from the hierarchy into employees' private lives.

Through the empirical study presented in Chapter 70, we discovered two types of relations that are not included in the figure, even though they are a resource for breaking management rules. These are professional relations through which professional rules emerge, and relations between worker and client that give rise to service rules. They have yet to be worked into the model depicted in Figure 71.1. Both professional and client relations would be represented by arrows going into the hierarchy from outside, as a source of resistance. Further, I only take the power hierarchy of command into consideration. There are, of course, other contradictions and hierarchies at workplaces about which it is possible to find narratives and theories in social science analyses of organizational misbehaviour. One concerns another aspect of the relation between service workers and customers in that the intricacies of dealing with managers have their counterparts in the niceties of relating to difficult customers or getting tips. Then there is the gender hierarchy: how do women deal with and resist patriarchal power at workplaces? Further, there are ethnic hierarchies: how do ethnically segregated people struggle to attain dignity in and at work? But these topics are for later – for now, back to organizational misbehaviour and resistance.

Resistance

A final remark, however, before discussing the concepts of the model. I will be quite generous in providing examples, both from the narratives of Part II and new ones, and the reason for this is that I want to illustrate the point of departure for the model: resistance, abusive supervision, collective discipline and private business are all different subsets of organizational misbehaviour. Each illustration is an example of organizational misbehaviour and, at the same time, of one of the other concepts in question.

Ackroyd and Thompson (1999: 163–5) say that organizational misbehaviour and resistance are different concepts; misbehaviour directs the searchlight towards areas that resistance has neglected, thus filling a gap. This claim is given more substance when Collinson and Ackroyd (2005: 306) explain that there is a conceptual continuum

> of oppositional workplace practices ranging from resistance (with connotations of behaviour that is overt, principled, and perhaps formally organized), through misbehaviour (defined as self-conscious rule-breaking), to dissent (which foregrounds linguistic or normative disagreement).

I strongly underscore that the concept of organizational misbehaviour, in the version of Ackroyd and Thompson, has had an enormously fruitful impact on this field of research. Yet, in my analysis, the relationship between the terms looks quite different: organizational misbehaviour is the overriding concept and resistance constitutes a subset thereof. The reason for this is that although the general approach of Ackroyd and Thompson is that organizational misbehaviour is a social relation rather than specific activities, they place it in a continuum that is a mix of these opposing conceptual principles. Overt behaviour is, for example, a type of behaviour independent of social relations, rule-breaking is part of the relationship between management and workers, and linguistic disagreement is, again, an activity in itself. At the same time, it seems to me that both resistance and dissent are, in this formulation, conscious rule-breaking and thus really parts of misbehaviour. I suggest that it is more fruitful for empirical research in this area to take its point of departure in a typology that systematically builds on the social relations of the power hierarchy in workplaces.

It is probably natural that those engaged in the British debate on resistance and organizational misbehaviour emphasize the differences between concepts and approaches. Still, it has surprised me a little that the debate does not seem to have led to anyone changing his or her mind. I have not been able to find anyone saying to an opponent: 'I was wrong on that point and you were right.' From my point of view as a stranger (Simmel, 1950), the debate is less of a debate than trench warfare. My approach is, instead, to look at possible relationships between some of the concepts mentioned in the debate. I disregard, however, some extreme positions; for example, resistance being either trivial or impossible (Contu, 2008), or that it is a shortcoming to conceptualize resistance as actions rather than identities and subject positions (Thomas and Davies, 2005).

Let us start with the term 'resistance'. This points, then, to a subset of organizational misbehaviour. The definition I wish to put forward is this: 'resistance is anything you consciously are, do and think at work that you are not supposed to be, do and think, and which is directed upwards through the organizational hierarchy'. Resistance is a form of organizational misbehaviour that is a response by employees to employer control – a response that tries to establish and maintain autonomy and dignity. Researchers do not agree, however, on what is meant by the term. Rose Weitz (2001: 669) even sees reason to complain about the fact that it 'remains loosely defined, allowing some scholars to see it almost everywhere and others almost nowhere'. An underlying theme in most definitions (cf. Hollander and Einwohner 2004; Seymore, 2006), however, is that which is now part of the concept of organizational misbehaviour: resistance is intentional, and the purpose of actions, thoughts and identity is to oppose the power of superiors with the aim of influencing the frontier of control in the contested terrain of the workplace in favour of the subordinates. In this way, they try to establish dignity at work. The source of rules for breaking these rules can vary, as we saw among the Norwegian health care workers. The most important source is some kind of informal self-organization or collectivity among employees.

Here is a tale of resistance that we recognize from Chapter 56 (Taylor and Bain, 2004: 289):

> The dress code changed and we were told, 'You have to wear a shirt and tie'. So we got word around, 'Tomorrow, wear shirts and ties that make us look as unprofessional as possible'. I wore a tie about four or five inches wide, illustrating the history and future of the motor car in glorious technicolour, along with a purple-checked shirt. Everybody dressed like this and there was nothing management could do.

One formulation of the definition of resistance is 'directed upwards through the hierarchy', which means that the actions, thoughts and identities can exist wherever you are located within the hierarchy: there is always someone higher up. And there is a lot of resistance going on within management, among managers on different levels. A classic example that sociologists seldom consider, since it is regarded to belong to political science, is senior officials' potential resistance to ministers of government departments (Barker and Wilson, 1997). Perhaps a more familiar example from industry is presented in Chapter 19 and concerns plant managers' resistance to corporate management. One of the plant managers summarized what happened thus (Taplin, 2001: 17):

> They (corporate) wanted gains in productivity, costs, quality and improved flexibility. Teams were meant to do this but often the opposite occurred. So we changed the emphasis of teams to meet productivity goals, cut supervision and forced workers to pay more attention to quality. In the last couple years we've done quite well ... But the big thing is that I'm able to deliver key numbers at the end of the year. The CFO is happy although I must admit there's a lot of creative accounting going on.

The plant managers resisted the corporate managers' intentions, leading to poorer results for the corporation but better bonuses for the plant managers.

Resistance is a form of organizational misbehaviour that is directed upwards through workplace hierarchies. As such, it is a way of defending the employees' dignity when it is threatened.

Abusive supervision

In the literature on bullying and harassment in the workplace, there is a specialism concerning 'abusive supervision', that is, downwards hostility of different types (Tepper, 2007). I want to pick up on this term, but I will also define it in relation to organizational misbehaviour. By 'abusive supervision', I mean 'anything you consciously are, do and think at work that you are not supposed to be, do and think, and that is directed downwards through the hierarchy'. Most work organizations have explicit and formal rules against all forms of bullying – often expressed as 'zero tolerance', which means that abusive supervision is a form of rule-breaking.

Much of the literature on abusive supervision is psychological, concentrating on what is called the abusive boss, or the boss from hell, described as 'one whose primary objective is the control of others, and such control is achieved through methods that create fear and intimidation' (Bies and Tripp, 1998: 205). Abusive bosses are obsessed with perfection, which is shown in extremely high expectations regarding performance; if these are not met, it will always be the subordinates' fault, never that of the boss. Their moods swing unpredictably between calm and violent outbursts. They demand loyalty and strict obedience from their subordinates. Dissenters are severely punished; for example, by being reprimanded in front of others. They achieve control over their subordinates by 'creating fear and intimidation and creating confusion and disorientation' (210).

The management literature, however, is conspicuously taciturn on the topic: it is a 'black hole' (Rayner and Cooper, 2003) in its analyses. Nevertheless, the sociology of work literature and ethnology literature is full of examples of managers bullying junior managers and of junior managers bullying workers. Still, it is difficult to find studies revealing which rules abusive managers draw on when breaking the general management rule against bullying. My hypothesis is that those rules emanate from informal relations with more senior managers, allowing, or perhaps even encouraging, abusive supervision. There are good arguments that abusive supervision in workplaces is endemic to the wage labour relation as such, although this can take different empirical forms, including a relative lack of bullying, depending on social context (Beale and Hoel, 2011).

It is also difficult to find reliable information about the extent of abusive supervision in workplaces, but it seems clear that it is a widespread phenomenon. It has, for example, been estimated that 75 per cent of all bullying in workplaces takes the form of downward hostility (Tepper, 2007: 267). In a survey of shop-floor workers at the British GM and BMW/Rover car plants, this question was posed: 'Do you feel bullied at work?' To this, 10 per cent said they felt bullied by a fellow worker, 14 per cent by a team leader and 29 per cent by a manager (Stewart et al., 2009: 191). It seems that abusive supervision is the most common form of bullying in workplaces, although some Nordic countries might be exceptions in that bullying is more common among workers (Beale and Hoel, 2011: 6).

What does abusive supervision look like, in concrete terms? This fairly mild example comes from a factory (Cavendish, 1982: 97):

> Tweedledum, Tweedledee and the other managers seemed like cardboard characters, and we thought them rude and bad mannered. Even if they stopped right by you or took the UMO [the product] out of your hand, they acted as if you weren't there. If they went through the heavy rubberised swing doors into the main assembly in front of you, they let them swing back on you, which no worker would ever do... They had so little respect for the workers that they couldn't even admit we existed.

This is a comment from a car worker (Stewart et al., 2009: 192):

> Managers don't really show a lot of respect nowadays. It's a different culture because managers may be under pressure too. I mean I'm not making excuses for them, because they take their pressure out on the shopfloor. We've had instances where people have been spoken to in terrible situations, where people have got sworn at, and apart from physically hitting somebody, it's the worse kind of abuse that you can get – you know, harassment. They don't even get rapped over the knuckles. If it was you or me you'd lose your job.

But abusive supervision is not confined to industry shop floors. The following story is about a manager in an office (Hornstein, 1996: 5):

> 'Billy,' he said, standing in the doorway so that everyone in the central area could see and hear us clearly. 'Billy, this is just not adequate, really not at all. We want to do better than this.' He was speaking very slowly and quietly, as if I were a three-year-old. As he spoke he crumpled the papers that he held. My work. One by one he crumpled the papers, holding them out as if they were something dirty and dropping them just inside my office as everyone watched.
>
> Then he said loudly, 'Garbage in, garbage out.' I started to speak, but he cut me off. 'You gave me garbage. Now you clean it up.'
>
> I did. Through the doorway I could see people looking away because they were embarrassed for me. They didn't want to see what was in front of them: a thirty-six-year-old man in a three-piece suit stooping before his boss to pick up crumpled pieces of paper.

Finally, it is worth noting that abusive supervision may also lead to resistance from those who are being subjected to the treatment. An example of this is provided in Chapter 42, which is set in a nightclub and concerns the replacement of broken security shutters (Analoui and Kakabadse, 1989: 37):

> Once new shutters were installed – following injuries to two of the clients – the managers laid down new rules as to how they should be operated. The General Manager, pointing to the new shutters, proclaimed: 'Those shutters cost 1,000 quid, more than all of you are worth. I can replace you lot anytime I wish, but I can't afford those shutters again. Make sure that they're not dropped on the counters.' It was interesting to see that the very participants who had insisted on the replacement of the old and dangerous shutters were now pulling the heavy steel shutters down so vigorously that they were soon rendered useless. As one employee pointed out: 'If the shutters are worth more than me (workers) do you wonder how much exactly we are each worth...down with the shutters...'

Abusive supervision is a form of organizational misbehaviour that is directed downwards through workplace hierarchies and that directly threatens the dignity of its victims.

Collective discipline

One of the most important concepts in Ackroyd and Thompson's analysis is 'self-organisation', by which they mean (1999: 54) 'the tendency of groups to form interests and establish identities and to develop autonomy based on these activities'. This combination of self-identity and self-interest forms the basis of employee resistance in the workplace.

In turn, self-organization leads, I would suggest, to a special type of organizational misbehaviour: collective discipline within the self-organized group. And, of course, all self-organization is misbehaviour. 'Collective discipline' is 'anything you consciously are, do and think at work which you are not supposed to be, do, and think, and which is directed laterally through the hierarchy in order to maintain discipline in self-organized groups'. This is not management-induced collective discipline but the internal discipline that is necessary for self-organized groups to act collectively. Ostracism, for example, is a common way of punishing aberrant members of self-organized groups. That was the type of discipline used on a worker in Chapter 12 (based on McKinley and Taylor, 1996; 1998) dealing with the struggle against the peer-review system at the Factory of the Future. Collective resistance had started to emerge and, when this worker broke the collective discipline, the other workers stopped talking to him, so he quickly started complying with the norms of self-organization.

Another term for self-organization is worker or employee collectivity. In connection with studies of lean production, Paul Stewart and colleagues have presented a terminology concerning collectivities in working life (Martinez Lucio and Stewart, 1997; Stephenson and Stewart, 2001). One of the terms is 'workplace collectivism', defined as 'the willingness on the part of employees to provide support for each other in the workplace around either work or non-work issues' (Stephenson and Stewart, 2001: 6.8). Another contribution is Alan Fox's (1971) analysis of the 'employee collectivity', which can exist among the 'lower participants' of work organizations. In spite of that it can have a rather large geographical extension: 'The relevant collectivity may be either the immediate work group, the wider work group, the trade union's local organization, or the union's national organization – or some combination of these' (1971: 92). In the introductory chapter, I referred, finally, to Lysgaard's (2001) theory of the 'worker collectivity', which concerns employees at the bottom of the workplace hierarchy but does not include unions. The collectivity is a buffer against the insatiability, one-sidedness and implacability of the technical-economic system of the work organization. Being employees, workers are necessarily part of this system, but the worker collectivity provides them with *protected* 'membership' of the technical-economic system.

All these types of collectivities are, under different descriptions, self-organizations for defending workers' dignity; their activities are misbehaviour in the form of resistance. As this is a collective endeavour, internal discipline is necessary to uphold common action. The most developed analysis of this phenomenon can be found in the theories of the employee collectivity and the worker collectivity. The discipline has two grounds: one is to keep workers in line with collective norms, the other to make all workers comply with informal agreements made with management. Part of the interaction between workers is not just spontaneous, therefore, but controlling in nature by means of inspecting, rewarding and punishing behaviour in relation to collective norms. One of the workers in Lysgaard's (2001: 114, my translation) study has this to say about workers who have been punished:

If they have been burned, they become more careful, of course. They can get a suggestion from the others to pull themselves together. We can agree to freeze him out...there are not many who can stand that pressure, it is very effective.

Fox (1971: 119) explains that in work-group collectivities 'social pressures towards conformity range through a finely graded series of the almost imperceptible to the extreme severity of complete ostracism'. The punishments for breaking collectivity rules involve constantly being met with hostility, being despised and losing all dignity. Those who are sanctioned are sanctioned by all worker groups in the workplace, all backs are turned, all conversations stop, all networks become closed units and anyone being friendly receives the same treatment.

The norms include not doing more or less work than collectively decided on and not aspiring to become a foreman. One of the strongest norms is not to have any more than is absolutely necessary to do with superiors, which is part of the sharp distinction made between 'us down here' and 'them up there'. Here is an empirical example of when a foreman stops to talk to a worker (Thompson, 1983: 222):

> The worker would be smiling and conversing congenially, yet the moment the foreman turned to walk away, the worker would make an obscene gesture (usually involving the middle finger) behind the foreman's back, so that all workers could clearly see.

In that way, the worker made it very clear that he dissociated himself from the foreman by giving the message 'I belong to us, not them.' The strength of the collectivity, as well as its own hierarchy of positions, is impressed on new workers from day one. This is an example from a slaughterhouse (Ackroyd and Crowdy, 1990: 6):

> Younger and weaker members of the team would often be subjected to extreme pressures by more experienced or skilled men. One recurrent example of this was an aspect of normal work performance, in which the completion of work would be used to harass certain workers. This possibility arose because the speed of the line tended to be set by the average speed of all, leading to a build-up of work at the stations of the slower men. Attempting to work faster than the next man was an objective every worker would aim at if the opportunity arose, and for the more experienced and skilled it arose on a regular basis. When it was achieved it would be accompanied by a rising tide of comment on the inferior performance and general inadequacy of the operative in difficulty.

The collectivity provides employees with '*power* and *honour* in a situation where they would individually be both powerless and without honour' (Lysgaard, 2001: 147; original emphasis; my translation) – in other words, the collectivity protects the workers' dignity. At the same time, it does so by enforcing its norms to such an extent that it can threaten the dignity of workers who deviate. Like abusive supervision, internal disciplining in collectivities can take the form of bullying.

Private business

Some organizational misbehaviour does not emanate from the workplace. Employees are more than employees – they have a life outside work, too. That part of their lives is also active during working hours – employees engage in private activities at work. 'Private business' is 'anything you consciously are, do and think at work that you are not supposed to be, do and think, and that is directed outwards from the hierarchy'. Recently, the boundary between work and life outside work has been expanding as a research theme: how can people make their professional and private lives fit together when the demands of both spheres seem to be growing (e.g. Warhurst et al., 2008)? It is an aspect of this that we are dealing with here: things that employees do, think about and are at work but that are of a private nature. One's private life can intrude on work, allowing private business to disturb one's work, or perhaps even take precedence over it. Although these questions are part of a flowering research area, private business at work remains a rather unknown phenomenon in the social sciences. However, it has recently come to the attention of management consultants due to the costs involved for employers; thus, enormous sums have been mentioned. There are calculations from the United States that have resulted in, for example, the estimate that employees watching basketball at work cost $3.8 billion in lost productivity, that water-cooler conversations about the Super Bowl cost up to $821.4 million and that internet surfing cost billions of dollars annually (D'Abate, 2005: 1011–12). Often, these calculations are made by consultancy firms, however, which simultaneously offer solutions to these problems.

In the literature on organizational misbehaviour and resistance, we catch glimpses every now and then of private activities, mostly concerning specific types of private business. Two examples of this are industrial employees making things at work for private use and 'cyber loafing' in the office (Lim, 2002). In the most comprehensive recent study of the first case, Michel Anteby (2008: 30) says that the American term is 'making homers', while the British one is 'pilfering'. One could add that in Gouldner's (1954) classic American study, the phenomenon is called 'government job'. The terminological problem, however, is more complex than Anteby claims. Pilfering is a much broader concept than homer making, while the British meaning of homer making is wider than the one that Anteby indicates. In connection with the present model I will, however, stick to Anteby's term homer making, which he defines as (2008: 29) 'a worker's use of company materials or tools in his or her workplace, during working hours, to manufacture or transform articles that are not part of the official production of the organization'. A more exhaustive formulation can be found in Linhart's (1982: 92, my translation) definition of the French equivalent, *perruques*: 'Utilizing breaks, slack periods or when you are ahead of production in order to manufacture utility goods or handicrafts using one's tools, the machine one has access to or discarded materials which one takes from the firm.' In examples of homers from Hungary, France and the United States, Anteby (34–5) mentions key chains, ashtrays, necklace charms, daggers, knives, bath mats, children's dolls, vases, firearms, kitchen cabinets, miniature aircraft engines, lamps and motorcycle parts. I can personally add two Swedish items to this catalogue: for my summer cottage, a friend of mine who is a welder made steps from the jetty into the lake and a weather vane in steel in the shape of an elk.

In Anteby's study, the workers do not regard making homers as the theft of company materials or time. One of his interviewees said (78): 'Homers are made by people who know how to craft artefacts. Theft is negative. These people are builders. Even though we used materials, we never stole anything. This is not theft – take note of that. It is craftsmanship.' Homer making is officially prohibited by the corporate code of conduct, but it is sometimes accepted by supervisors and even by managers higher up in the hierarchy. At the same time, it does happen that workers discovered in the act of making homers are punished with suspension or even dismissal. The ambiguous way homers are treated by management is perhaps most obvious when managers order workers to make homers for them. The workers cannot refuse, but they do not regard this as proper homer making, rather as an ordinary job. Workers make homers for their own homes, for friends or as gifts to workmates who are retiring.

Among office employees, there are few possibilities of making homers, but here is a catalogue of the types of private business they conduct (D'Abate and Eddy, 2007: 364–5):

Using the telephone for personal reasons, surfing the Internet, sending and receiving personal e-mail, having social conversations, making appointments, reading for leisure, placing bets or engaging in betting pools, watching TV, playing computer games, downloading music, paying bills, shopping online, and getting visits from family and friends during work hours are all examples of how home and leisure can cross the boundaries of work and enter into the workday.

The most comprehensive study so far of office employees, conducted by Caroline P. D'Abate (2005) in the United States, is based on interviews with 30 middle managers. All of them occupied themselves with private matters during working hours, with the most common activities including making private phone calls, sending or reading emails, talking about things that were not work-related and surfing the internet. In answer to the question about why they did these things, three reasons emerged as the most common ones. The first was simply that it was convenient. The phone and the computer were there, ready to be used. The second was that these managers always had to live with time pressure. It would be very difficult to make life outside work function in a reasonably smooth way if they were unable to use part of their working hours for private business. One of them said (D'Abate, 2005: 1024): 'You know it's the only way I've been able to balance a career and a personal life. If I weren't able to do things at work, then I probably wouldn't be able to stay working.' The third reason was in order to be able to adjust to the opening times of various organizations, which were only open during normal working hours; for example, mechanics and doctors.

It is obvious that private business involves actions and thoughts, but does it also include identity? The results indicate that this is the case, as can be seen in this comment made by one of the interviewees (D'Abate, 2005: 1024):

> I would say that [I do home and leisure type activities] to not forget about them during the workday ... to recognize that everything is not all about work ... in this day and age, oftentimes work is so all-encompassing that it's easy to forget about the other things in your life, and I think it's healthy to incorporate those other areas that make you the person that you are that comes to work every day.

This middle manager clearly emphasizes the fact that they regard it as important not just to be the person required by the job; on the contrary, it is crucial to take the identity anchored in home and leisure into work. The interviewees let things belonging to life outside work invade their work because it is meaningful and important for them to do so. It is a part of their dignity. In doing so, they draw on rules anchored outside the workplace, which they allow to override management rules.

Anteby (2008) claims that management allows a great deal of homer making in exchange for workers' consent. It is not quite clear how this function is achieved, other than being part of 'grey zones' in the workplace: 'areas in which workers and their supervisors together engage in practices that are officially forbidden, yet tolerated by the organization' (139–40). This indicates, I would suggest, that private business generally has to be tolerated to some extent by management as part of the struggle regarding the frontier of control; this means that there is no absolute borderline, thus constituting a grey zone.

Conclusion

In the existing empirical research, the phenomena I have mentioned are usually analysed as separate entities lacking any connection with each other. I suggest that fruitful empirical studies could also be conducted by analysing the relationships between organizational misbehaviour, resistance, abusive supervision, collective discipline and private activities. The reason I have returned to so many empirical examples is that I wanted to indicate that they are all instances of organizational misbehaviour – but that, at the same time, they can be regarded as separate examples of the different subsets of misbehaviour. What holds them together is their relationship with the hierarchy of command at the workplace; the distinctions between them are constituted by the different directions they take in relation to this hierarchy.

Studies of organizational misbehaviour are always of vital importance because people need dignity and autonomy at work. If they are denied dignity and autonomy, there will be a strong tendency for them to resist their working conditions.

Notes

38 The Docile and Loyal Cleaners

1. The following is part of an article by Lundberg and Karlsson (2011) 'Under the Clean Surface – Working as a Hotel Attendant' *Work, Employment and Society*, 25(1), pp. 141–48. I am grateful to the publishers, Sage, for permission to reproduce it in this form.

46 The Academics' Real Work

1. I am taking the opportunity to write these sentences at 6.30 a.m. on a Saturday, while keeping a grandchild company watching a cartoon on TV.

70 Organizational Misbehaviour

1. This section is an abridged version of a paper by Kirchhoff and Karlsson (2009) 'Rationales of Breaking Management Rules – the Case of Health Care Workers' *Journal of Workplace Rights* 25(1), pp. 457–79. I am grateful to the publishers, Baywood Publishing Company, for permission to reproduce it in this form.

References

Ackroyd, Stephen and Peter Crowdy (1990) 'Can Culture Be Managed? Working with "Raw" Material: The Case of the English Slaughtermen' *Personnel Review* 19(5), pp. 3–13.

Ackroyd, Stephen and Paul Thompson (1999) *Organizational Misbehaviour* London: Sage.

Analoui, Farhad and Andrew Kakabadse (1989) 'Defiance at Work' *Employee Relations* 11(3), pp. 2–62.

Anderson, Gina (2006) 'Carving out Time and Space in the Managerial University' *Journal of Organizational Change Management* 19(5), pp. 578–92.

Anderson, Gina (2008) 'Mapping Academic Resistance in the Managerial University' *Organization* 15(3), pp. 251–70.

Anteby, Michel (2008) *Moral Grey Zones: Side Production, Identity, and Regulation in an Aeronautic Plant* Princeton: Princeton University Press.

Aronson, Jane and Sheila M. Neysmith (1996) ' "You're Not Just in There to Do the Work" Depersonalizing Policies and the Exploitation of Home Care Workers' Labour' *Gender and Society* 10(1), pp. 59–77.

Badham, Richard, Karin Garrety, Viviane Morrigan, Michael Zanko and Patrick Dawson (2003) 'Designer Deviance: Enterprise and Deviance in Culture Change Programmes' *Organization* 10(4), pp. 707–30.

Baldamus, Wilhelm (1967) *Efficiency and Effort: An Analysis of Industrial Administration* London: Tavistock.

Balser, Deborah B. and Robert N. Stern (1999) 'Resistance and Cooperation: A Response to Conflict Over Job Performance' *Human Relations* 52(8), pp. 1029–53.

Barker, Anthony and Graham K. Wilson (1997) 'Whitehall's Disobedient Servants? Senior Officials' Potential Resistance to Ministers in British Government Departments' *British Journal of Political Science* 27(2), pp. 223–46.

Barnes, Alison (2007) 'The Construction of Control: The Physical Environment and the Development of Resistance and Accommodation within Call Centres' *Work, Technology and Employment* 22(3), pp. 246–59.

Bayard de Volo, Lorraine (2003) 'Service and Surveillance: Infrapolitics at Work Among Casino Cocktail Waitresses" *Social Politics* 10(3), pp. 346–76.

Baxter, Vern and Steve Kroll-Smith (2005) 'Normalizing the Workplace Nap: Blurring the Boundaries between Public and Private Space and Time' *Current Sociology* 53(4), pp. 387–403.

Beale, David and Helge Hoel (2011) 'Workplace Bullying and the Employment Relationship: Exploring Questions of Prevention, Control and Context' *Work, Employment and Society* 25(1), pp. 5–18.

Bélanger, Jacques and Christian Thuderoz (2010) 'The Repertoire of Employee Opposition' in Paul Thompson and Chris Smith (eds) *Working Life. Renewing Labour Process Analysis* Basingstoke: Palgrave Macmillan.

Bergman, Paavo and Rune Wigblad (1999) 'Workers Last Performance: Why Some Factories Show Their Best Results During Countdown' *Economic and Industrial Democracy* 20(3), pp. 343–68.

Bies, Robert J. and Thomas M. Tripp (1998) 'Two Faces of the Powerless. Coping with Tyranny in Organizations' in Roderick M. Kramer and Margaret A. Neale (eds) *Power and Influence in Organizations* London: Sage.

Bolton, Sharon C. (2004) 'A Bit of a Laugh: Nurses' Use of Humour as a Mode of Resistance' in Mike Dent, John Chandler and Jim Barry (eds) *Questioning the New Public Management* Aldershot: Ashgate.

Bolton, Sharon C. (2007) 'Dignity *in* and *at* Work: Why It Matters' in Sharon C. Bolton (ed.) *Dimensions of Dignity at Work* Amsterdam: Butterworth-Heinemann.

Bolton, Sharon C. (2010) 'Being Human: Dignity of Labor as the Foundation for the Spirit–Work Connection' *Journal of Management, Spirituality and Religion* 7(2), pp. 157–72.

Braddock, Jeremy and Stephen Hock (2001) 'The Specter of Illegitimacy in an Age of Disillusion and Crisis' in Jeremy Braddock and Stephen Hock (eds) *Directed by Allen Smithee* Minneapolis: University of Minnesota Press pp. 3–27.

Brower, Ralph S. and Mitchel Y. Abolfia (1995) 'The Structural Embeddedness of Resistance among Public Managers' *Group and Organization Management* 20(2), pp. 149–66.

Bunge, Mario (1998) *Social Science Under Debate: A Philosophical Perspective* Toronto: University of Toronto Press.

Burawoy, Michael (1979) *Manufacturing Consent. Changes in the Labor Process under Monopoly Capitalism* Chicago: University of Chicago Press.

Burchell, Brendan J. (2002) 'The Prevalence and Redistribution of Job Insecurity and Work Intensification' in Brendan J. Burchell, David Lapido and Frank Wilkinson (eds) *Job Insecurity and Work Intensification* London: Routledge.

Button, Graham, David Mason and Wes Sharrock (2003) 'Disempowerment and Resistance in the Print Industry? Reactions to Surveillance-Capable Technology' *New Technology, Work and Employment* 18(1), pp. 50–61.

Carls, Kristin (2007) 'Affective Labour in Milanese Large Scale Retailing: Labour Control and Employees' Coping Strategies' *Ephemera: Theory and Politics in Organization* 7(1), pp. 46–59.

Carls, Kristin (2009) 'Coping with Control? Retail Employee Responses to Flexibilisation' *Qualitative Research in Accounting and Management* 6(1/2), pp. 83–101.

Cavendish, Ruth (1982) *Women on the Line* Boston: Routledge and Kegan Paul.

Collinson, David (1994) 'Strategies of Resistance: Power, Knowledge and Subjectivity in the Workplace' in John M. Jermier, David Knights and Walter R. Nord (eds) *Resistance and Power in Organizations* London: Routledge pp. 25–68.

Collinson, David and Stephen Ackroyd (2005) 'Resistance, Misbehaviour, and Dissent' in Stephen Ackroyd, Rosemary Batt, Paul Thompson and Pamela S. Tolbert (eds) *The Oxford Handbook of Work and Organization* Oxford: Oxford University Press pp. 305–26.

Contu, Alessia (2008) 'Decaf Resistance. On Misbehaviour, Cynicism, and Desire in Liberal Workplaces' *Management Communication Quarterly* 21(3), pp. 364–79.

Cooke, Hannah (2006) 'Seagull Management and the Control of Nursing Work' *Work, Employment and Society* 20(2), pp. 223–43.

Cully, M., S. Woodland, A. O'Reilly and G. Dix (1999) *Britain at Work: As Depicted by the 1998 Workplace Employee Relations Survey* London: Routledge.

Cushen, Jean (2009) 'Branding Employees' *Qualitative Research in Accounting and Management* 6(1/2), pp. 102–114.

D'Abate, Caroline P. (2005) 'Working Hard or Hardly Working: A Study of Individuals Engaging in Personal Business on the Job'' *Human Relations* 58(8), pp. 1009–32.

D'Abate, Caroline P. and Erik R. Eddy (2007) 'Engaging in Personal Business on the Job: Extending the Presenteeism Construct' *Human Resource Development Quarterly* 18(3), pp. 361–83.

Danermark, Berth, Mats Ekström, Liselotte Jakobsen and Jan Ch. Karlsson (2002) *Explaining Society: Critical Realism in the Social Sciences* London: Routledge.

Dent, Erik B. and Susan Galloway Goldberg (1999) 'Challenging "Resistance to Change"' *Journal of Applied Behavioral Science* 35(1), pp. 25–41.

Devinatz, Victor G. (2007) 'Manufacturing Resistance: Rationalizing the Irrationality of Managerial Control on the Shop Floor in a US Medical Electronics Factory' *Employee Responsibility and Rights Journal* 19(1), pp. 1–15.

Ditton, Jason (1979) 'Baking Time' *The Sociological Review* 27(1), pp. 157–67.

Edwards, P. K. (1986) *Conflict at Work. A Materialist Analysis of Workplace Relations* Oxford: Basil Blackwell.

Edwards, Paul, David Collinson and Giuseppe Della Rocca (1995) 'Workplace Resistance in Western Europe: A Preliminary Overview and a Research Agenda' *European Journal of Industrial Relations* 3(1), pp. 283–316.

Edwards, Paul, Jacques Bélanger and Martyn Wright (2006) 'The Bases of Compromise in the Workplace: A Theoretical Framework' *British Journal of Industrial Relations* 44(1), pp. 125–45.

Edwards, Richard (1979) *Contested Terrain* New York: Basic Books.

Egan, R. Danielle (2004) 'Eyeing the Scene: The Uses and (Re)uses of Surveillance Cameras in an Exotic Dance Club' *Critical Sociology* 30(2), pp. 299–319.

Egan, R. Danielle (2006) 'Resistance under the Black Light. Exploring the Use of Music in Two Exotic Dance Clubs' *Journal of Contemporary Ethnography* 35(2), pp. 201–19.

Ezzamel, Mahmoud, Hugh Willmot and Frank Worthington (2001) 'Power, Control and Resistance in "The Factory that Time Forgot"' *Journal of Management Studies* 38(8), pp. 1053–79.

Ezzamel, Mahmoud, Hugh Willmot and Frank Worthington (2004) 'Accounting and Management–Labour Relations: The Politics of Production in the "Factory with a Problem"' *Accounting, Organizations and Society* 29(3–4), pp. 269–302.

Felstead, Alan, Duncan Gallie and Francis Green (2004) 'Job Complexity and Task Discretion: Tracking the Direction of Skills at Work in Britain' in Chris Warhurst, Irena Grugulis and Ewat Keep (eds) *The Skills that Matter* Basingstoke: Palgrave Macmillan pp. 148–69.

Fenton-O'Creevy, Mark (1998) 'Employee Involvement and the Middle Manager: Evidence from a Survey of Organizations' *Journal of Organizational Behavior* 19(1), pp. 67–84.

Fine, Gary Alan (1996) *Kitchens: The Culture of Restaurant Work* Berkeley: University of California Press.

Fleetwood, Steve (2008) 'Institutions and Social Structures' *Journal for the Theory of Social Behaviour* 38(3), pp. 241–65.

Fleming, Peter (2005a) 'Workers' Playtime? Boundaries and Cynicism in a "Culture of Fun" Program' *The Journal of Applied Behavioral Science* 41(3), pp. 285–303.

Fleming, Peter (2005b) '"Kindergarten Cop": Paternalism and Resistance in a High-Commitment Workplace' *Journal of Management Studies* 42(7), pp. 1469–89.

Fox, Alan (1971) *A Sociology of Work in Industry* London: Collier-Macmillan.

Freeman, Richard B. and Joel Rogers (2006) *What Workers Want* Ithaca, New York: ILR Press.

Friedman, Andrew L. (1977) *Industry and Labour* London: Macmillan.

Fuller, Linda and Vicki Smith (1991) 'Customers' Reports: Management by Customers in a Changing Economy' *Work, Employment and Society* 5(1), pp. 1–16.

Furåker, Bengt (2005) *Sociological Perspectives on Labor Markets* Basingstoke: Palgrave Macmillan.

Goodrich, Carter L. (1975 [1920]) *The Frontier of Control* London: Pluto.

Gouldner, Alvin W. (1954) *Patterns of Industrial Bureaucracy*, New York: Free Press.

Graham, Laurie (1993) 'Inside a Japanese Transplant. A Critical Perspective' *Work and Occupations* 20(2), pp. 147–73.

Graham, Laurie (1995) *On the Line at Subaru-Isuzu. The Japanese Model and the American Worker* Ithaca, NY: ILR Press.

Green-Pedersen, Christoffer (2002) 'New Public Management Reforms of the Danish and Swedish Welfare States: The Role of Different Social Democratic Responses' *Governance: An International Journal of Policy, Administration, and Institutions* 15(2), pp. 271–94.

Gurley Flynn, Elizabeth (1997 [1916]) 'Sabotage: The Conscious Withdrawal of the Workers' Industrial Efficiency' in Salvatore Salerno (ed.) *Direct Action and Sabotage. Three Classic IWW Pamphlets from the 1910s* Chicago: Charles H. Kerr pp. 98–115.

Hannigan, B. (1998) 'Assessing the New Public Management: The Case of the National Health Service' *Journal of Nursing Management* 6(5), pp. 307–12.

Hansen, Inger Lise B. (2007) '*Arbeiderkollektivet – 50 år etter?'* *Masteroppgave.* Halden: Avdeling for samfunnsfag og fremmedspråk, Høgskolen i Østfold.

Hansson, Magnus (2008) *On Closedowns: Towards a Pattern of Explanations to the Closedown Effect* Örebro: Business Studies, Örebro University.

Harris, Lloyd C. and Emmanuel Ogbonna (2006) 'Service Sabotage: A Study of Antecedents and Consequences' *Journal of Academy of Marketing Science* 34(4), pp. 543–58.

Herbst, Philip G. (1971) 'Utviklingen av sosio-teknisk analyse' in Philip G. Herbst (ed.) *Demokratiseringsprosessen i arbeidslivet* Oslo: Universitetsforlaget pp. 11–18.

Hochschild, Arlie Russell (2003) *The Managed Heart. Commercialization of Human Feeling* Berkeley: University of California Press.

Hodson, Randy (1991) 'The Active Worker. Compliance and Autonomy at the Workplace' *Journal of Contemporary Ethnography* 20(1), pp. 47–78.

Hodson, Randy (1995) 'Worker Resistance: An Underdeveloped Concept in the Sociology of Work' *Economic and Industrial Democracy* 16(1), pp. 79–110.

Hodson, Randy (2001) *Dignity at Work* Cambridge: Cambridge University Press.

Hodson, Randy (2002) 'Demography or Respect? Work Group Demography Versus Organizational Dynamics as Determinants of Meaning and Satisfaction at Work' *British Journal of Sociology* 53(2), pp. 291–317.

Hoffman, Elizabeth A. (2008) ' "Revenge" and "Rescue": Workplace Deviance in the Taxicab Industry' *Sociological Inquiry* 78(3), pp. 270–89.

Hollander, Joycelyn A. and Rachel L. Einwohner (2004) 'Conceptualizing Resistance' *Sociological Forum* 19(4), pp. 533–54.

Hornstein, Harvey A. (1996) *Brutal Bosses and Their Prey* New York: Riverhead.

Hutchinson, Sally (1990) 'Responsible Subversion: A Study of Rule Bending Among Nurses' *Scholarly Inquiry for Nursing Practice: An International Journal* 4(1), pp. 3–17.

Huzell, Henrietta (2005) *Management och motstånd. Offentlig sektor i omvandling – en fallstudie* Karlstad: Karlstad University Press.

Huzell, Henrietta (2009) 'Striving for Flexibility, Attaining Resistance: Culture Clashes in the Swedish Rail Industry' in Egil J. Skorstad and Helge Ramsdal (eds) *Flexible Organizations and the New Working Life. A European Perspective* Farnhem: Ashgate pp. 163–85.

Judge, Timothy A., Carl J. Thoresen, Joyce E. Bono and Gregory K. Patton (2001) 'The Job Satisfaction–Job Performance Relationship: A Qualitative and Quantitative Review' *Psychological Bulletin* 127(3), pp. 376–407.

Karasek, Robert A. (1979) 'Job Demands, Job Decision Latitude, and Mental Strain: Implications for Job Redesign' *Administrative Science Quarterly* 24(2), pp. 285–308.

Karasek, Robert and Töres Theorell (1990) *Healthy Work. Stress, Productivity, and the Reconstruction of Working Life* New York: Basic Books.

Karlsson, Jan Ch. (2004) 'The Ontology of Work. Social Relations and Doing in the Sphere of Necessity' in Steve Fleetwood and Stephen Ackroyd (eds) *Critical Realist Applications in Organisation and Management Studies* London: Routledge pp. 90–112.

Karner, Tracy X. (1998) 'Professional Caring: Homecare Workers as Fictive Kin' *Journal of Ageing Studies* 12(1), pp. 69–82.

Kirchhoff, Jörg W. (2010) *De skjulte tjenestene – om uønsket adferd i offentlige organisasjoner* Karlstad: Karlstad University Press.

Kirchhoff, Jörg W. and Jan Ch. Karlsson (2009) 'Rationales of Breaking Management Rules – The Case of Health Care Workers' *Journal of Workplace Rights* 14(4), pp. 457–79.

Knights, David and Darren McCabe (1998) ' "What Happens When the Phone Goes Wild?": Staff, Stress and Spaces for Escape in a BPR Telephone Banking Work Regime' *Journal of Management Studies* 53(2), pp. 163–94.

Korczynski, Marek (2007) 'Music and Meaning on the Factory Floor' *Work and Occupations* 34(3), pp. 253–89.

Kousha, Mahnaz (1994) 'African American Private Household Workers and "Control" of the Labor Process in Domestic Service' *Sociological Focus* 27(3), pp. 211–28.

Lankshear, Gloria, Peter Cook, David Mason, Sally Coates and Graham Button (2001) 'Call Centre Employees' Responses to Electronic Monitoring: Some Research Findings' *Work, Employment and Society* 15(3), pp. 595–605.

Lawson, Tony (2003) *Reorienting Economics* London: Routledge.

Lim, Vivien K. G. (2002) 'The IT Way of Loafing on the Job: Cyberloafing, Neutralizing and Organizational Justice' *Journal of Organizational Behavior* 23(5), pp. 675–94.

Linhart, Danièle (1982) 'Au-delà de la norme. A propos de la créativité ouvrière' *Culture et technique* (8), pp. 91–8.

Linhart, Robert (1978) *L'etabli* Paris: Ed. De Minuit.

Linstead, Stephen and Robert Grafton-Small (1992) 'On Reading Organizational Culture' *Organization Studies*, 13(3) pp. 331–55.

Lundberg, Helena and Jan Ch. Karlsson (2011) 'Under the Clean Surface – Working as a Hotel Attendant' *Work, Employment and Society* 25(1), pp. 141–48.

Lysgaard, Sverre (2001 [1961]) *Arbeiderkollektivet* Oslo: Universitetsforlaget.

Major, Maria and Trevor Hopper (2005) 'Managers Divided: Implementing ABC in a Portugese Telecommunications Company' *Management Accounting Research* 16(2), pp. 205–29.

Martin, Randy (1986) 'Sowing the Threads of Resistance: Worker Resistance and Managerial Control in a Paint and Garment Factory' *Humanity and Society* 10(3), pp. 259–75.

Martinez Lucio, Miguel and Paul Stewart (1997) 'The Paradox of Contemporary Labour Process Theory: The Rediscovery of Labour and the Disappearance of Collectivism' *Capital and Class* 62, pp. 49–77.

Marx, Karl (1998) *Capital. Vol. I* London: ElecBook.

Maslyn, John M., Steven M. Farmer and Donald B. Fedor (1996) 'Failed Upward Influence Attempts. Predicting the Nature of Subordinate Persistence in Pursuit of Organizational Goals' *Group and Organization Management* 21(4), pp. 461–80.

McKinlay, Alan and Phil Taylor (1996) 'Power, Surveillance and Resistance: Inside the "Factory of the Future" ' in Peter Ackers, Chris Smith and Paul

Smith (eds) *The New Workplace and Trade Unionism* London: Routledge pp. 279–300.

McKinlay, Alan and Phil Taylor (1998) 'Through the Looking Glass: Foucault and the Politics of Production' in Alan McKinlay and Ken Starkey (eds) *Foucault, Management and Organization Theory from Panopticon to Technologies of Self.* London: Sage pp. 173–90.

Morgan, Gareth (1986) *Images of Organization* London: Sage.

Morrison, Elizabeth W. (2006) 'Doing the Job Well: An Investigation of Pro-social Rule Breaking' *Journal of Management* 32(1), pp. 5–28.

Mulholland, Kate (2004) 'Workplace Resistance in an Irish Call Centre: Slammin', Scammin', Smokin' an' Leavin' ' *Work, Employment and Society* 18(4), pp. 709–24.

Næss, Sturle (2003) *I tøffeste laget – Dokumentasjonsrapport om arbeidssituasjonen til ansatte i pleie- og omsorgstjenesten* Bergen: Rokkansenteret, Rapport 9/2003.

Napier, Brian (1972) 'Working to Rule – A Breach of the Contract of Employment?' *The Industrial Law Journal* 1(1), pp. 125–34.

O'Connell Davidson, Julia (1994) 'The Sources and Limits of Resistance in a Privatized Utility' in John M. Jermier, David Knights and Walter R. Nord (eds) *Resistance and Power in Organizations* London: Routledge pp. 69–101.

O'Day, Rory (1974) 'Intimidation Rituals: Reactions to Reform' *The Journal of Applied Behavioral Science* 10(3), pp. 373–86.

Ong, Aihwa (1987) *Spirits of Resistance and Capitalist Discipline. Factory Women in Malaysia* Albany: State University of New York Press.

Paules, Greta Foff (1991) *Dishing It Out: Power and Resistance among Waitresses in a New Jersey Restaurant.* Philadelphia: Temple University Press.

Pollert, Anna (1981) *Girls, Wives, Factory Lives* London: Macmillan.

Pollert, Anna and Andy Charlwood (2009) 'The Vulnerable Worker in Britain and Problems at Work' *Work, Employment and Society* 23(2), pp. 343–62.

Prasad, Anshuman and Pushkala Prasad (1998) 'Everyday Struggles at the Workplace: The Nature and Implications of Routine Resistance in Contemporary Organizations' *Research in the Sociology of Organizations* 15, pp. 225–57.

Prasad, Anshuman and Pushkala Prasad (2001) '(Un)willing to Resist? The Discursive Production of Local Workplace Opposition' *Studies in Cultures, Organizations and Societies* 7(2), pp. 105–25.

Prasad, Pushkala and Anshuman Prasad (2000) 'Stretching the Iron Cage: The Constitution and Implications of Routine Workplace Resistance' *Organization Science* 11(4), pp. 387–403.

Ramsdal Helge and Gunnar Vold Hansen (2005) 'Om sirkelens kvadratur – Psykisk helsearbeid møter bestiller-/utførerorganisasjonen' *Tidsskrift for psykisk helsearbeid* 2(2), pp. 134–48.

Rasmussen, Bente (2004) 'Between Endless Needs and Limited Resources: The Gendered Construction of a Greedy Organization' *Gender, Work and Organization* 11(5), pp. 506–25.

Rayner, Charlotte and Cary L. Cooper (2003) 'The Black Hole in "Bullying at Work" Research' *International Journal of Management and Decision Making* 4(1), pp. 47–64.

Richards, James and Abigail Marks (2007) 'Biting the Hand that Feeds: Social Identity and Resistance in Restaurant Teams' *International Journal of Business Science and Applied Management* 2(2), pp. 42–57.

Roberts, John (1984) 'The Moral Character of Management Practice' *Journal of Management Studies* 21(3), pp. 287–302.

Roethlisberger, F.J. and William J. Dickson (1965 [1939]) *Management and the Worker* New York: John Wiley and Sons.

Roy, Donald (1955) 'Efficiency and "the Fix": Informal Intergroup Relations in a Piecework Machine Shop' *American Journal of Sociology* 60(2), pp. 255–66.

Sallaz, Jeffrey J. (2002) 'The House Rules. Autonomy and Interests among Service Workers in the Contemporary Casino Industry' *Work and Occupations* 29(4), pp. 394–427.

Sayer, Andrew (2007a) 'Dignity at Work: Broadening the Agenda' *Organization* 14(4), pp. 565–81.

Sayer, Andrew (2007b) 'What Dignity at Work Means' in Sharon C. Bolton (ed.) *Dimensions of Dignity at Work* Amsterdam: Butterworth-Heinemann pp. 17–29.

Seymore, Susan (2006) 'Resistance' *Anthropological Theory* 6(3), pp. 303–21.

Sharpe, Diana Rosemary (2006) 'Shop Floor Practices under Changing Forms of Managerial Control: A Comparative Ethnographic Study of Micropolitics, Control and Resistance within a Japanese Multinational' *Journal of International Management* 12(5), pp. 318–39.

Simmel, Georg (1950) 'The Stranger', in Kurt H. Wolff (ed.) *The Sociology of Georg Simmel* New York: Free Press.

Simonet, Daniel (2008) 'The New Public Management Theory and European Health-Care Reform' *Canadian Public Administration* 51(4), pp. 617–35.

Skorstad, Egil J. (2002) *Organisasjonsformer. Kontinuitet eller forandring?* Oslo: Gyldendal Akademisk.

Smith, Chris (2006) 'The Double Indeterminacy of Labour Power: Labour Effort and Labour Mobility' *Work, Employment and Society* 20(2), pp. 389–402.

Smith, Vicki (1990) *Managing in the Corporate Interest. Control and Resistance in an American Bank* Berkeley: University of California Press.

Stephenson, Carol and Paul Stewart (2001) 'The Whispering Shadow: Collectivism and Individualism at Ikeda-Hoover and Nissan UK' *Sociological Research Online* 6(3).

Stewart, Paul, Mike Richardson, Andy Danford, Ken Murphy, Tony Richardson and Vicki Wass (2009) *We Sell Our Time No More. Workers' Struggles against Lean Production in the British Car Industry* London: Pluto Press.

Strauss, George (1955) 'Group Dynamics and Intergroup Relations' in William Foote Whyte: Money and Motivation New York: Harper and Row pp. 90–6.

Strömberg, Susanne and Jan Ch. Karlsson (2009) 'Rituals of Fun and Mischief: The Case of the Swedish Meatpackers' *Employee Relations* 31(6), pp. 632–47.

Taplin, Ian M. (2001) 'Managerial Resistance to High Performance Workplace Practices' in Steven P. Vallas (ed.) *Research in the Sociology of Work, Vol. 10. The Transformation of Work* Amsterdam: JAI pp. 1–24.

Taylor, Phil and Peter Bain (2003) ' "Subterranean Worksick Blues": Humour as Subversion in Two Call Centres' *Organization Studies* 24(9), pp. 1487–509.

Taylor, Phil and Peter Bain (2004) 'Humour and Subversion in Two Call Centres' in Steve Fleetwood and Stephen Ackroyd (eds) *Critical Realist Applications in Organisation and Management Studies* London: Routledge pp. 274–97.

Taylor, Steve (1998) 'Emotional Labour and the New Workplace' in Paul Thompson and Chris Warhurst (eds) *Workplaces of the Future* Basingstoke: Macmillan pp. 84–103.

Tepper, Bennett J. (2007) 'Abusive Supervision in Work Organizations: Review, Synthesis, and Research Agenda' *Journal of Management* 33(3), pp. 261–89.

de Terssac, Gilbert (1992) *Autonomie dans le travail* Paris: PUF.

Thomas, Robyn and Annette Davies (2005) 'Theorizing the Micro-politics of Resistance: New Public Management and Managerial Identities in the UK Public Services' *Organization Studies* 26(5), pp. 683–706.

Thompson, Paul and David McHugh (2009) *Work Organisations. A Critical Approach* Basingstoke: Palgrave Macmillan.

Thompson, William E. (1983) 'Hanging Tongues: A Sociological Encounter with the Assembly Line' *Qualitative Sociology* 6(3), pp. 215–37.

Thorsrud, Einar and Fred E. Emery (1970) 'Industrial Democracy in Norway' *Industrial Relations* 9(2), pp. 187–96.

Timmons, Stephen (2003) 'Nurses Resisting Information Technology' *Nursing Inquiry* 10(4), pp. 257–69.

Townsend, Keith (2004) 'Management Culture and Employee Resistance: Investigating the Management of Leisure Service Employees' *Managing Leisure* 9(1), pp. 47–58.

Vabø, Mia (2005) 'New Public Managment i nordisk eldreomsorg – hva forskes det på?' pp. 73–111 in Marta Szebehely (ed.), *Äldreomsorgsforskning i Norden.* Köpenhamn: Nordiska Ministerrådet.

Vabø, Mia (2007) *Organisering for velferd. Hjemmetjenester i en styringsideologisk brytningstid.* Oslo: Oslo university.

Vallas, Steven P. (2003) 'The Adventures of Managerial Hegemony: Teamwork, Ideology, and Worker Resistance' *Social Problems* 50(2), pp. 204–25.

Vredenburgh, Donald and Yeal Brender (1998) 'The Hierarchical Abuse of Power in Work Organizations' *Journal of Business Ethics* 17(12), pp. 1337–47.

Warhurst, Chris, Doris Ruth Eikhof and Axel Haunschild (eds) (2008) *Work Less, Live More? A Critical Analysis of the Work-life Boundary.* Basingstoke: Palgrave Macmillan.

Warren, Sam and Stephen Fineman (1997) "'Don't Get Me Wrong, It's Fun Here, but …" Ambivalence and Paradox in a "Fun" Work Environment' in Robert Westwood and Carl Rhodes (eds) *Humour, Work and Organization* London: Routledge pp. 92–112.

Webb, Mike and Gerry Palmer (1998) 'Evading Surveillance and Making Time: An Ethnographic View of the Japanese Factory Floor in Britain' *British Journal of Industrial Relations* 36(4), pp. 611–27.

Weitz, Rose (2001) 'Women and Their Hair: Seeking Power through Resistance and Accommodation' *Gender and Society* 15(5), pp. 667–86.

White, Caroline (1988) 'Why Do Workers Bother? Paradoxes of Resistance in Two English Factories' *Critique of Anthropology* 7(3), pp. 51–71.

Wiklund, Per (2007) *Kampen för människovärdet. Om identitet i ett föränderligt arbetsliv* Stockholm: Karolinska institutet.

Wilkinson, Michael J. (1995) 'Love Is Not a Marketable Commodity: New Public Management in the British National Health Service' *Journal of Advanced Nursing* 21, pp. 980–87.

Winters, Janet (2008) ' "We Can't Join a Union, that Would Harm the Horses": Worker Resistance in the UK Horseracing Industry' *Centre for Employment Studies Research Review* April 2008. www.uwe.ac.uk/bbs/research/cesr/review. shtml. (Accessed at 29 September 2010.)

Zhang, Xiaodan (2008) 'Hidden Forms of Bargaining on China's Shop Floor' *International Labor and Working-Class History* 73(1), pp. 7–23.

Zlolniski, Christian (2003) 'Labor Control and Resistance of Mexican Immigrant Janitors in Silicon Valley' *Human Organization* 62(1), pp. 39–49.

Index

209